The Sewing Connection Series III

by Shirley Adams

Copyright © 1991
Shirley Adams Publications
922 Cheltenham Way
Plainfield, IN 46168

All rights reserved. No part of this book may be reproduced in any form or by any means without the prior written consent of the author.

Printed in the United States of America

Table of Contents

1. Reversibles.
Using both sides of a fabric together or at times, just the flip side.
Two faced fabrics and reversible garments are shown. 1

2. Matching Magic.
Plaids and stripes are big news. Where to begin and how to proceed
are demonstrated for a perfect match. 6

3. Come Rain or Come Shine.
Rainwear is explored from waterproof to water repellant. Some season
extenders are shown to warm up lightweight outerwear. 9

4. Sweatering.
Handling of sweater bodies or sweater yardage is demonstrated.
Edging varieties are applied when no finished edge is provided. 13

5. One Layer Coats . . . Interior.
Suitable fabrics are used without facings, interfacings, or linings.
Alternatives in seams and fastenings are shown. 17

6. On The Edge.
Once the coat's interior is complete, techniques and findings to finish
the edges are shown in a wide variety. 21

7. Altering Manmade Suedes.
Gained or lost a little weight? Don't panic as suede garments can be
let out or taken in whether the seams were conventional or lapped.
A zipper is inserted without a seam. 29

8. Distorting The Facts.
Very simple shapes take on a more sophisticated air when cut up
and rearranged in appliques. 33

9. Create a Collar.
A mere neckline measurement is the basis for designing a collar.
Overlapping shoulder front and back will give the precise shape of a
fitted collar. 39

10. *Turtle Quilt.*
    The quilt that folds up and stores itself inside its own attached pillow cover is a delight for a child's nap cover or a family room lap robe.   42

11. *Make It Special.*
    No one needs one more garment just to cover up in! Make everything distinctive, original, creative to mark it as your own.   46

12. *Little Black Dress.*
    A staple in any wardrobe, a neutral colored basic can go in any direction to suit your need just adding accessories.   49

13. *Night On The Town.*
    Beginning with the #12 basic, a multitude of treatments are possible to create a festive air. Among them are trims, stitching variations, jackets or stoles to turn day into night.   53

Many thanks to:

David Larson Productions
5910 North Lilly Road
Menomonee Falls, WI 53051

Dave and Kate, producers,
models Christina Larson and Kathy Thompson,
director-editor Ivy Lynn Revolinski, Jeff Cartier,
David C. Larson, Jim Lillis, Peter Pfankuch,
Tom Reardon, Mary Reidinger, Andy Stieber.
photographer Marty Savasta.
Also models Rebecca Adams and Beverly Evans

Special thanks to:

Viking Sewing Machine Co.
11750 Berea Road
Cleveland, OH 44111

Program 1: Reversibles

Welcome back to The Sewing Connection for Series III. The idea behind all these programs is that you can have anything you want ON YOUR TERMS if you sew. Sewing is YOUR connection to the world of fashion.

The central theme behind series III is THE FLIP SIDE ... the alternatives when one way fails. Or what happens when you turn your thinking around, backwards, inside out? Have you ever bought a disc or a tape for a particular number and discovered you liked the flip side even better? This series is the same idea. Sometimes reverses are planned and at other times they happen unexpectedly to surprise and delight you. Serendipity is a wonderful reward for keeping an open mind and allowing little miracles to unfold.

The jacket on the book cover began as most projects do for me ... slowly browsing a nice fabric shop. Never dash in and out of those treasure houses hurriedly as you might miss all the best they offer! A leisurely stroll allows you to hear one bolt say "Here I am!" As you carry it around the shop, another and yet a third and fourth jump out as the obvious, the irresistible companion fabrics for mix and match wardrobe building.

This particular day as I circled around all the counters I repeatedly came back to one bolt, a tapestry of enormous and very bold tulips. Woven in dramatically in great contrasts of darks and lights, I could envision a huge panel of this framed on a wall. But as a wearable article it was really overpowering. You must feel comfortable in your clothes. You wear them. They cannot dominate you.

The strong attraction continued and I finally opened the double layer to look at its back. There it was ... the flip side! On the wrong side with its softer nuances I could see many more wearable possibilities. Anyway, who's to say what's right and what's wrong? When you sew, you're the designer and you choose what you like.

In the final analysis, I possibly bought it because it was such a challenge. A whole lot of sewing is cerebral. It's the joy of envisioning what might be, then working through the thought processes of making it happen.

Because both sides of the fabric are fascinating might be a good reason to combine them both in one garment. Being able to see the contrast of the two sides at once could be quite interesting. Imagine, for example, the two faces of denim. Woven of dark warp yarns and white filling yarns, the outside shows up dark while the inside is much lighter. A way to combine the two sides follows.

Construct the garment laying together the wrong sides of adjoining pieces of fabric. Stitch the 5/8" seams and press them open with a steam iron. -sketch 1.1-

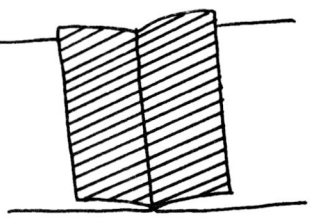

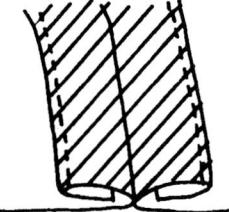

Press the edges under again, this time 14". Top stitch the outer folds down to the garment, resulting in the light fabric side outlining at all seams the major dark areas of the garment. -sketch 1.2-

The hem is pressed to the outside about 1" in depth. Then its edge is turned under and topstitched in place in a manner similar to the seam finishes. -sketch 1.3-

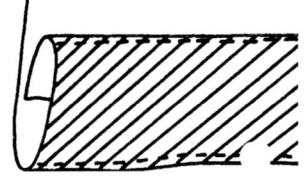

The final measurement of seams and hems stitched in place is about 5/8" to 3/4" wide. Make them the same.

This treatment takes care of most edges which are straight or very gently curved. But what will happen to drastically curved areas such as neckline or armscye seams? Obviously these seams with their inwardly curved smaller edges cannot be folded back into larger areas to stitch. -sketch 1.4- The answer here is adding an extra layer of fabric.

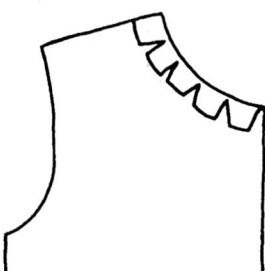

Cutting that strip on the bias is necessary for it to smoothly curve around edges. Its width should be a 5/8" seam allowance plus 5/8" stitched border which shows, plus a 1/4" turn under hem before stitching. This totals 1 1/2" and the length is as long as necessary to border its intended area.

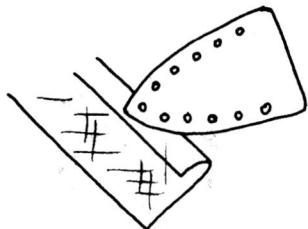

Press a 1/4" hem under (toward the dark side) all along one edge of the long strip. -sketch 1.5-

Remembering that this is to border a curve, it might be a good idea to pre-press this strip into a curve of the same shape before stitching it to the garment. As you proceed keep in mind the fact that bias stretches quite easily and as it becomes longer it also would become narrower. This narrowing you want to avoid since you are trying to keep all trims an equal width. As you press, therefore, condense the inner curve with the steam iron and the width will remain equal. Do not stretch out the outer curve. -sketch 1.6-

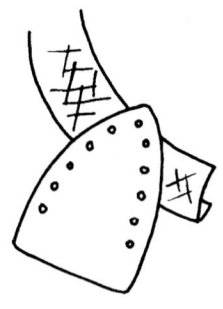

Around the neck edge decide in advance what will happen in the front corner. Do you prefer the neck band to overlap the front band as in sketch 1.7?

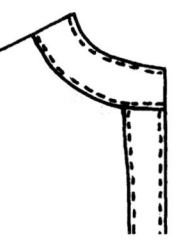

Or would you like them to meet in the middle as the mitered corner in sketch 1.8?

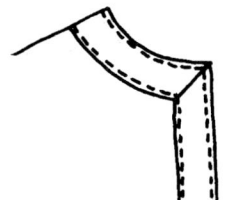

The third choice is for the front band to overlap the neck band as in sketch 1.9.

Plan in advance your completed look so you can decide which layer goes on first, then second, as you pin and stitch the corner area.

Basically what happens with the curved bias facings is that the right side of the facing (what you want to show when completed) is positioned against the wrong side of the garment neckline, as in sketch 1.10. Stitch the neck edge as shown up to what will be the corner.

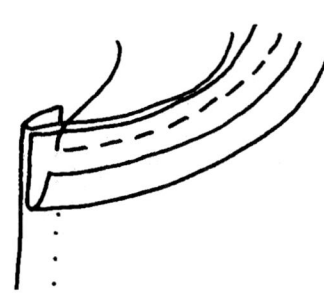

Grade (trim two seam allowances different sizes to layer or bevel) the neckline seam. Clip at 1/2" intervals so it will turn smoothly.

From there on it's a matter of folding one way or another the front band and the neck band according to which one you want on top in the finished look. Trim out anything bulky at the corner, press layers in place, top stitch and edge stitch to finish.

Around the armscye it might be easiest to
1. Stitch the garment shoulder.
2. Press under the bias strip 1/4" edge.
3. Press strip in a curve being careful to not stretch out of shape.
4. Pin and topstitch folded edge down to garment.-sketch 1.11-
5. Stitch underarm seam of garment.
6. Construct sleeve and set into armscye.

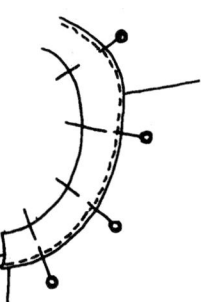

The finished jacket looks like sketch 1.12

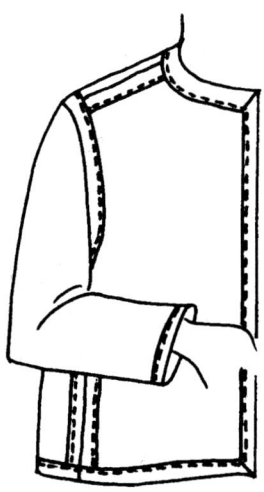

This would be a good way to do a solid fabric with a tonal reverse side such as denim. It would also be very attractive in a small print on one side, patterned weave on back side as the black and white print over the herringbone shown in program one. -sketch 1.13-

If covering curvy interior areas as shown in figure 1.13, a bias tape maker would be a very handy tool to use. This aids in folding under the raw edges, followed by an iron pressing it down as well as in curves. It is then easily topstitched in place on the garment.

Consider the same techniques using texture. For example, the smooth side of a leather-like fabric can be combined with its reverse side which has a suede roughness. Another good reverse in texture is crepe-back satin. The body of the blouse in sketch 1.14 with its many pleats is done on the crepe side showing the dull texture. The exterior facing around the neckline and down the front band is using the flip side of shiny satin. This use of the same color, but different play of light absorption or reflection produces an elegant contrast.

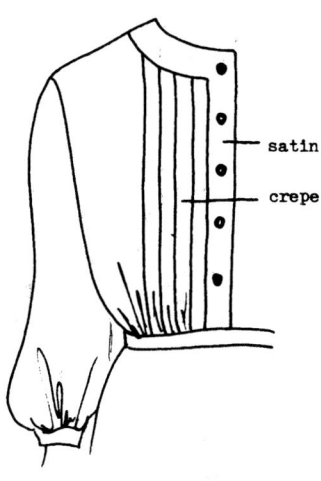

Many quilted fabrics on the market also have two faces of two different prints. Some have a print side and a solid side which can either be used combined to contrast areas, or to be used as a reversible garment. If used this way bind the edges with double fold bias tape made from another companion fabric.

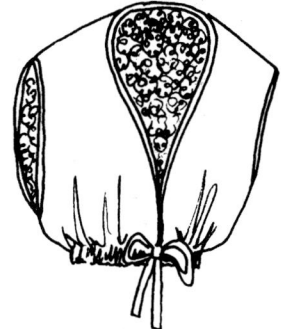

Simple garments such as the sketch 1.15 vest work out well done this way.

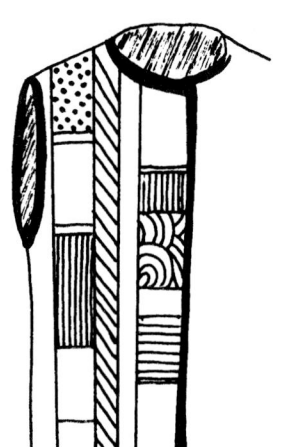
A vest with two sides, at least one of which you produce by piecing fabrics, is another possibility to explore. Sketch 1.16 illustrates an example. This would probably be finished by binding the edges together the same way. Or eliminating the binding, stitching layers together wrong sides out, then turning right side out is another choice.

Skirts, even raincoats can be made in this same way. For a wrap skirt make two complete skirts, sewing together the side seams on each. Right sides of the two skirts together, stitch around the ends and hem. -sketch 1.17- Turn it right side out through the open waist, 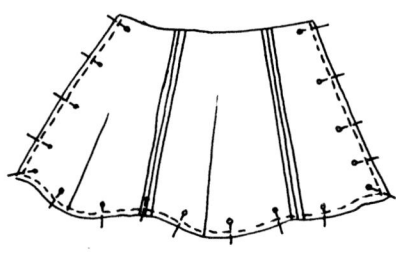 press the edges, attach it to a wrap-and-tie waistband. -sketch 1.18-

For a reversible raincoat, each layer would have its own pockets applied while in single layers (unless one is a slash and the other is a patch to conceal it). After the layers are stitched together, turned right side out, pressed and topstitched, the buttonholes and buttons are applied.

A double cloth is another really interesting adventure in dealing with the flip side. This is a heavy fabric woven with four distinct sets of yarns which cross over in a variety of designs (floral, geometric, etc.) locking the design outlines while reversing colors. This fabric must be seen to actually understand it. In working with it, the obvious solution would be to perfectly match the motifs wherever seams would occur. To cut at random would be quite ineffective and a waste.

After considering all these fabrics and their flip side possibilities, let's reconsider the cover tapestry fabric. Could it be used effectively combining the two sides? No, because of the large design, the multi-colors and its boldness it could not. The best way to use this is to choose a very simple pattern which has very few seams so the design will not be needlessly chopped up. To use it strikingly however, the colors forming muted stripes absolutely must be matched between sleeve and body of the jacket. Further, the tulip motif should run over a seam from one garment piece to the next if at all possible. The gauntlet has been flung! The challenge of this brainteaser is irresistible.

Matching the stripes at the side seams of garment front and back is deliciously simple. The fabric is wide enough to go around a medium sized body so by overlapping the pattern side seams at the stitching line, it is cut all in one piece. -sketch 1.19-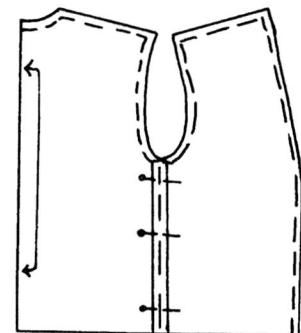

The next problem is the sleeve pattern placement. The obvious first step is that horizontal muted stripes, two inch groups of filling yarns must line up exactly right, NOT at the sleeve and armscye notches which may or may not match. The place to ALWAYS get a perfect match is at the underarm point X of sketch 1.20.

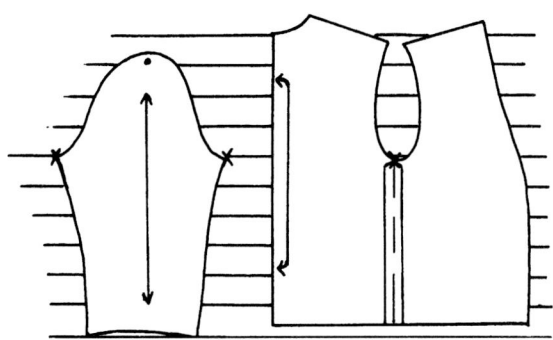

With the sleeve pattern on the correct horizontal stripe, it can then be moved left or right until the same flower joins sleeves with bodice for a perfect horizontal AND vertical match. -sketch 1.21- This is terrific mental exercise for the home sewer and an absolute delight when it works. Program 2 directs further matching.

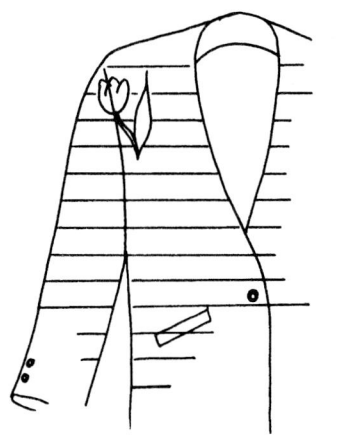

Sketch 1.21

Reversible raincoat, wrapskirt, and two vests courtesy of Sue Hausmann, education director of Viking Sewing Machine Company.

The silk denim suit courtesy of Mary Lee McCammack of Fine Line Fabrics in Coatesville, Indiana.

The pattern used was a Donna Karan by Vogue #2512, for both the jacket and the two-piece dress underneath shown on the book cover.

Program 2: Matching Magic

Plaids are big news this year so we better get our thinking ready for them. They really should be matched at every prominent joining for the greatest impact. Many other fabric designs, upon careful scrutiny, also need to be matched even though they are technically not plaids. A regular repeat horizontally and/or vertically tells you that matched, this garment would be better than a random cut.

The help you will get from your pattern guide sheet is negligible. Aside from telling you what pattern pieces will be needed in your chosen view, no other layout information is pertinent. The pattern manufacturer doesn't know you are using a fabric which needs to be matched. Other information such as the design repeat size as well as your body size are necessary input. Only you can put all these facts together. Then you can proceed as follows.

Hold the uncut fabric in front of your body as you stand before a mirror. Move it around until prominent stripes or motifs fall in graceful places. For example, if you would like to minimize your apparent hip size, bright colors should be moved elsewhere, with a somber stripe or design in places better left unnoticed. A huge cabbage rose looks better on a shoulder than right at the bust. Place a couple of pins in the fabric to mark where you want your bust, waist hip, center front, or whatever.

Is there a nap? This should smooth in the down direction. Has the fabric an identical right and wrong side? Or does a print definitely mark the right side? Can the fabric be folded and cut double? Or is it best cut one layer at a time? Even if this is a balanced plaid it may be quicker to cut single layers. To cut double, the two layers must be intricately adjusted and pinned every foot to be sure the verticals and horizontals are exactly coinciding.

Begin with the most important, the most prominent pattern piece ... the bodice front. You have already marked body locations on the fabric where the design would be most flattering, so simply lay the tissue where indicated. Do not initially pin to fabric as this may have to be moved and adjusted before the final layout is settled. Refer back to sketches 1.19 and 1.20 of chapter 1 to see if this overlapping of pattern pieces to cut the body as one will be possible. If the joining side seam is a straight line it can be overlapped with the stitching lines coinciding. The pattern will have to first be measured and if necessary, altered, because thus eliminating the side seams precludes any later fabric alterations. If the fabric measures smaller than your body, this cannot be done, and must be cut as separate back and fronts.

When positioning the two pattern pieces look for these things:
- Center front should be in the center of a vertical stripe if possible
- Center back should be in the center of a vertical stripe
- Side seams should be equidistant from a stripe so they blend together when stitched
- The side seams should be on the same horizontal level.

-Sketch 2.1- (see next page) has the back and front overlapped with the pattern pieces, print side up, laid on a single thickness fabric. The dotted lines indicate how the fabric would be flipped over to cut the second side after the first side is cut.

With the body pieces set, next be sure the sleeve will match. As in program 1, match the underarm points, not the notches -2.1 A (see next page). This sleeve has a high cap which stitches in

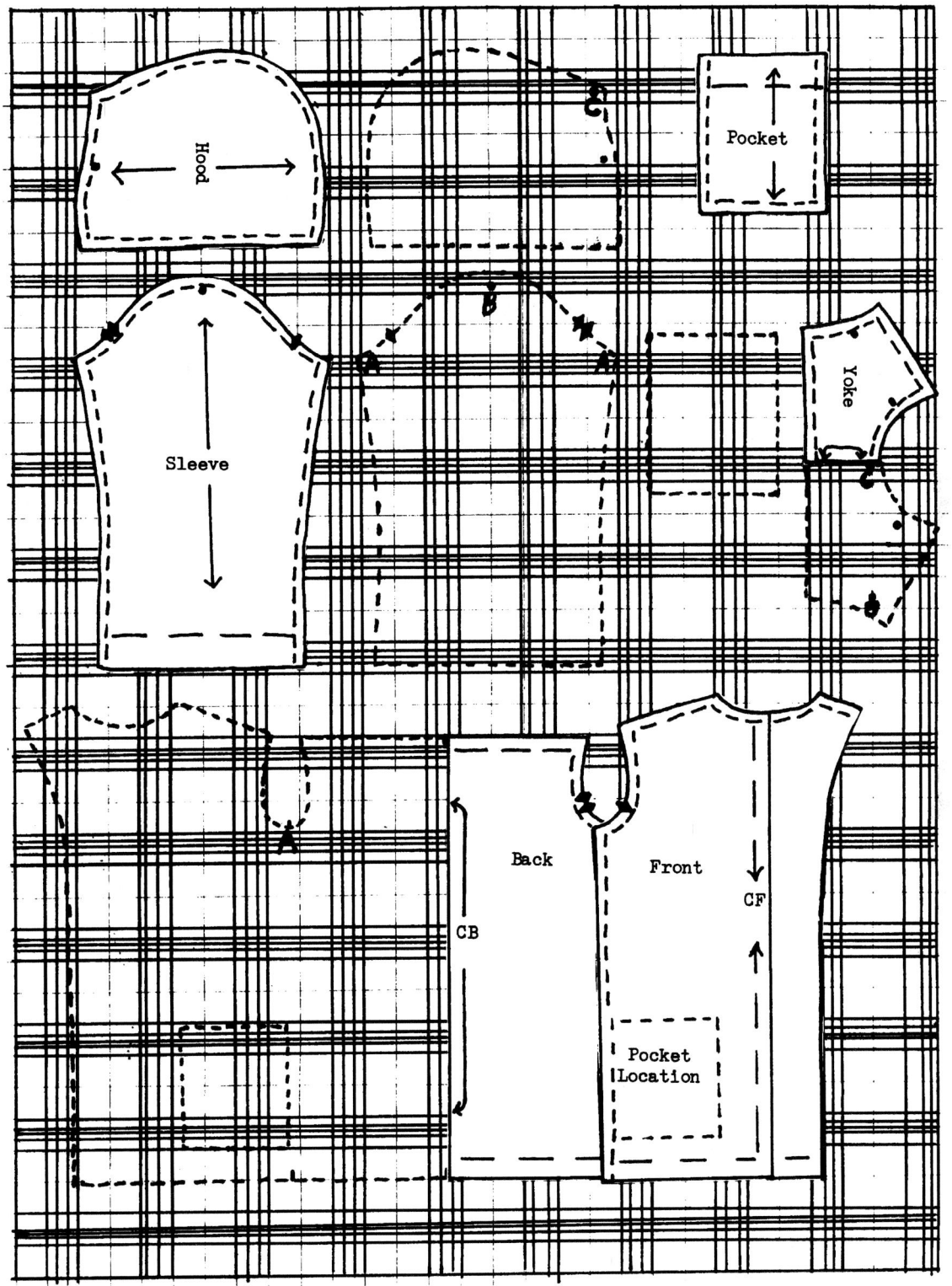

Sketch 2.1

near the shoulder point so it possibly would match regardless of whether one did notches or underarm points. But consider the shapes involved if the bodice had dropped shoulders. This always means that the sleeve cap will be flat, and notches then couldn't possibly match. -sketch 2.2-

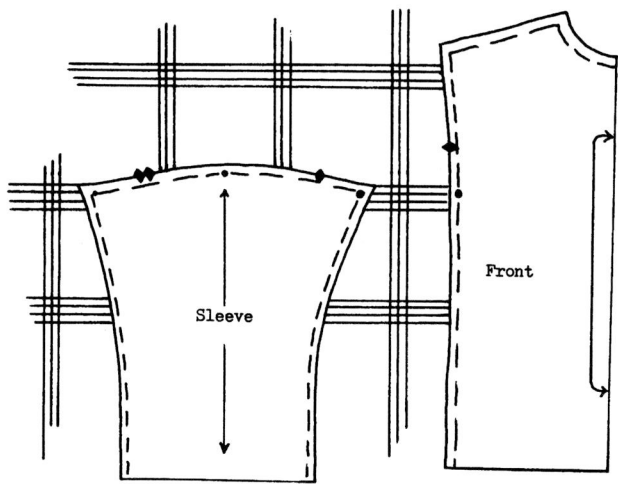

This illustrates why you can always depend on the underarm A points.

In producing a perfect sleeve-bodice match remember also that you should always avoid a horizontal dart at the bust. -sketch 2.3- This dart enables a match above or below, but not all over.

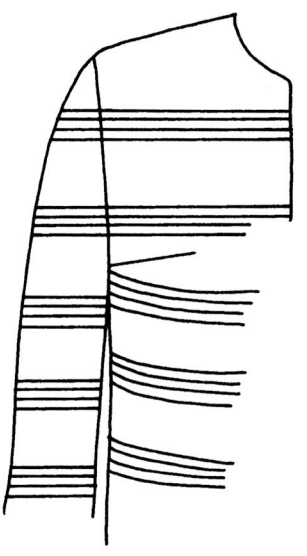

Once the sleeve level is ascertained by the underarm point, moving it right or left may be necessary for a vertical shoulder match. Reserve this decision until laying the shoulder yoke for that is what it will match. It would be nice to match the back yoke to the bodice back but to do so would throw the front yoke-bodice front completely off. The choice is therefore to put the yoke sideways or on the bias to purposely avoid it. Doing this puts the armscye shoulder point B in the center of a wide stripe. The sleeve center dot B is moved to the same spot.

The hood is turned sideways to match its center back lower dot to the yoke center neck back point C.

All that then remains is the patch pocket. The easiest way to match this so that it blends in perfectly is to position the pocket pattern on the correct spot of the plaid fabric and trace the plaid lines with a marker. Move the pocket pattern to an identical spot in the uncut fabric and cut out.

This was a fairly simple pattern making an anorak from an Indian blanket plaid. It was done to illustrate the logical thinking process which sets priorities and a workable process. From following the process it is hoped that you can then move into more difficult similar problems.

When assembling the jacket use lots of pins to hold stripes in place. An even feed or dual feed foot may help move the two layers equally.

Anorak pattern Vogue 7879

Program 3: Come Rain or Come Shine

The anorak pattern used in programs 2, or something similar, has another obvious use. When the threat of rain is present, it might be just the protection you'll need to wear as a casual cover-up to keep you dry.

The fabrics to look for are either waterproof or water repellent. The waterproof are coated to make them impenetrable. This coating may be a slick vinyl exterior such as is seen on slickers. At other times the coating is on the underside of the fabric and the right side is simply a woven cotton for casual wear or a dressy fabric when appropriate. Ultra Leather® and Ultra Suede® are also included in this classification. Unlike their animal counterparts, they will not be spotted or otherwise altered in appearance by getting wet. The nap on the suedes should go in the down direction so water more easily runs off. Do not use leather needles for any of these, as to cut slits every time the needle enters would permit water to also come through. Instead use a 70 - 80 stretch needle and longer stitch length. For some of these a Teflon foot is helpful for easier fabric movement.

The water repellent fabrics are a little more likely to eventually leak through. These are usually thin, very closely woven taffeta types of fabrics. Look for the micro fiber raincoating which is a rather new polyester fiber of an extremely fine denier. Again, it is closely woven to block out rain within reason. Some of the repellent fabrics are made more so by an aerosol spray which helps to fill in the tiny holes between yarns as well as filming over the fabric surface. This can be washed out so the effect is not permanent. Any of this type rainwear will eventually allow you to get some dampness through but if it is an absolute monsoon ... for goodness sake have the good sense to come in out of the rain!

Some of these fabrics feel a little clammy and would be more pleasant if they are lined. Something soft like a cotton flannel or a knit cotton interlock might be good linings in big casual jackets. If a long raincoat is lined a better choice might be a silky type lining fabric. If the styling is rather fitted and it will be worn over suits or dresses or sweaters, silky linings are also wise because of their slippery quality which permits easier movement.

Consider some the bright colors available. Not only do they give a mental lift but especially for children's rain gear, they offer a safety factor since they are easily seen on a dark grey day.

Lining, when no lining is included in the pattern, is an easy matter. It was explained in series II but here as a brief reminder is how. Because this garment is probably roomy, no ease pleat is needed at the center back. Because there are perhaps no shoulder pads, no changes are needed in shoulder seam or sleeve cap. Remember IF you have pads that the lining goes UNDER them so the lining shoulder seam and sleeve cap would taper down about 1/2" lower. -sketch 3.1-

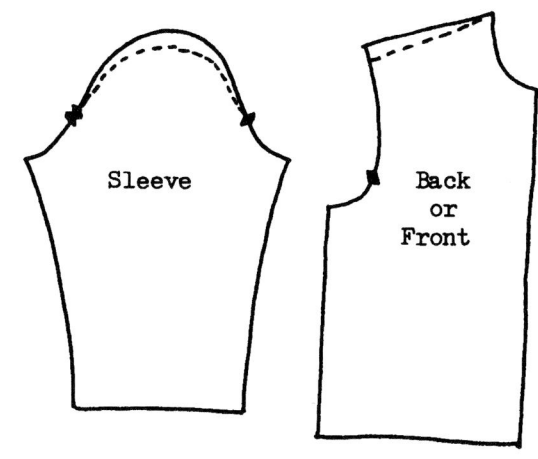

Other than that possibility, a basic lining is merely cut from the same pattern as the outer layers MINUS the facings, PLUS 1 1/4" (two seam allowances).

This is illustrated in sketch 3.2 and on the dotted lines is where the lining would be cut.

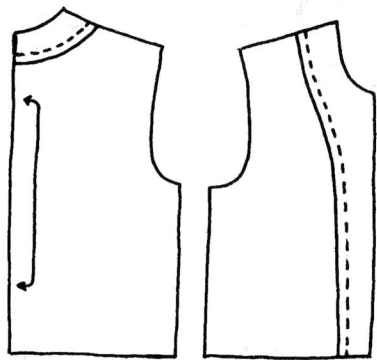

The facing edge is the solid line. The dotted line, 1 1/4" beyond, is the cutting line.

Then the lining edges are sewn to the facing edges, shoulder and side seams stitched and sleeves inserted. This whole unit is stitched around the outer edge to the jacket shell and turned right side out. There were the basics. Where your project may have variables is in hood or collar, zipper or buttons, drawstrings, pockets. Because of these other features, more explicit directions cannot be given without seeing your pattern.

Another possibility is eliminating the facings and bringing the lining fabric all the way out to the edges. In other words, it could be cut exactly the same as the fashion fabric layer ... especially if the lining fabric was something which could be used as a reversible.

Sometimes raincoats or rain jackets have extra features, extra partial layers. The military look is popular with epaulets on shoulders; buckled, buttoned or tied bands at wrists; extra shoulder protectors back and/or front.

Those extra layers as illustrated in figure 3.3 are simply duplicates of the garment piece they overlay, lower edges abbreviated.

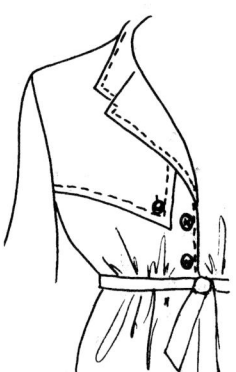

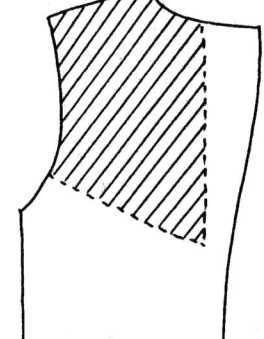

The pattern piece involved is shown in sketch 3.4. To cut the overlay use the pattern to cut the armscye, shoulder and part of the neck. Then remove the pattern and cut the rest of the dotted line on your own. It is advisable to "try on" the pattern in advance and looking in a mirror, mark where you will want those edges to end. Mark these on your fabric with chalk or pins and cut out adding seam allowances. This might be one layer of fabric whose lower edges are hemmed before staystitching it in place at armscye, shoulder and neck. Or it might be a double layer used with a lining fabric, seamed at the two loose edges and turned right side out, pressed, topstitched before staystitching to garment edges. Either way it will be an easy operation on which you cannot go wrong. A buttonhole and button are frequently added to hold the loose corner in place.

The raincoat back can be similarly treated to give a little military styling but mainly to add extra protection. Sketch 3.5 illustrates this possibility. When a center back pleat is

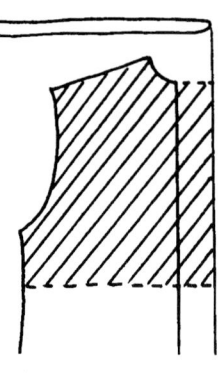 added to the overlay, sketch 3.6 of the pattern cutting is the easy way to do this. Notice how the pattern center back is not laid on the fabric fold in the usual way. It is instead positioned about 3 inches away from it, the extra fabric forming the pleat.

After cutting out the shaded part of upper pattern back, hem under the lower edge or seam it to a lining layer and turn right side out, press. Form a center back inverted pleat so that the neck edge of the overlay is the same as the garment back. Staystitch it in place at armscye, shoulder, and neck, then proceed with construction of the coat.

If you feel safer, a duplicate paper pattern could also be made and tried on the original.

The shoulder epaulets are made by measuring the pattern shoulder width including seam allowances. This will be the length of the band you cut times about 3 inches wide including seam allowances. Cut a double layer for each shoulder. Sketch 3.7 shows some ideas in attaching it to the garment.

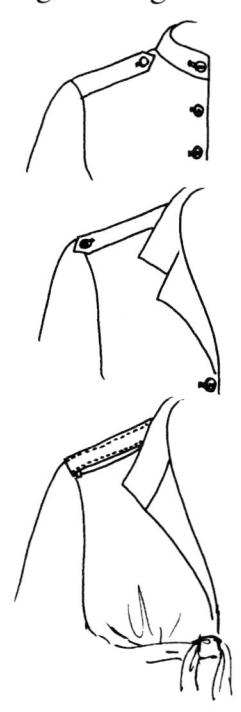

Epaulet stitched in sleeve seam, loose end buttoned near neck.

Epaulet stitched into neck seam, loose end buttoned out near sleeve.

Epaulet cut double length, both ends stitched into neck, small loop holding down center fold out at sleeve seam.

Sleeves may be trimmed at wrists with equal ease. Some possibilities for this are suggested in sketch 3.8.

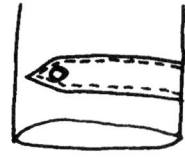

Double layers seamed, turned, pressed and topstitched. Raw ends are included in vertical sleeve seam, other end anchored with button.

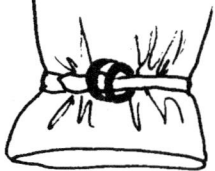

Narrower band is cut to go all around sleeve and fasten with double D rings. It is attached with stitches at the sleeve seam.

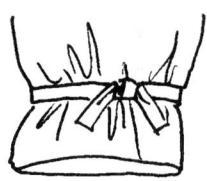

Long narrow band is tied in a small knot, also attached to coat at seam but held in place by little extra carriers.

A hood may be added to a jacket which hasn't one of its own. Trace this pattern on an 11" x 17" piece of paper, filling in the edge lines where the printer could not put them all on this page. It would come all the way out to the page edges. - sketch 3.9-

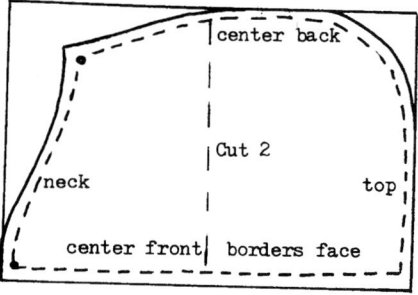

Measure your jacket neckline to see if it measures the same as this pattern neckline from the center front (CF) to the center back (CB). If any changes need to be made simply add or subtract whatever that is for a perfect fit at the center back.

This hood can be cut out of two fabric layers, stitched together with a flat felled seam at the back and top of the head, and hemmed on the straight line which surrounds the face. This can then be stitched into the neckline seam instead of a collar or, as a detachable hood, be buttoned on under the collar.

Another possibility for a detachable hood is to extend the season a little longer by adding a fur-lined hood to a purchased denim jacket. Shown on program 3 was such a hood made from this pattern but cutting two layers of manmade sheepskin for the lining layer. The outside denim layer was cut from some recycled denim which rather closely matched the color of the new stone-washed denim jacket. The source of the recycled denim was the cut off legs from the upside down jeans vest demonstrated in series I, program #9. Sketch 3.10- These legs were opened at the inner seam to produce flat fabric, the pattern laid and cut out.

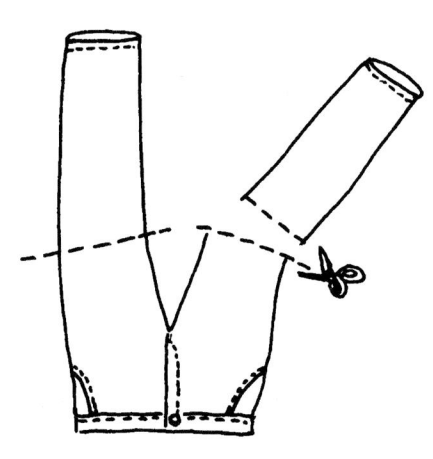

Stitch the two denim layers together at the center back with a heavy topstitching thread into a flat felled seam. Stitch the two fur layers together in a plain seam. Seam the two hoods together around the outer edges leaving a little space for turning right side out. Press edges carefully on denim side so as not to destroy fur layer. At neck edge of hood, spaced equidistant from each other, make four machine buttonholes. -sketch 3.11- Sew the corresponding four buttons under the jacket collar so the hood can be worn on or not.

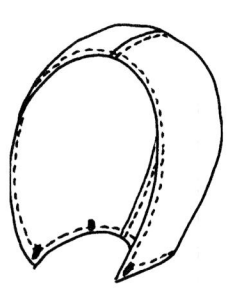

To make this stitching easier on the heavy layers of denim, be sure to use the special jeans needles. When approaching or stitching away from some of the multi-layered seams which must be crossed, use a button lift -sketch 3.12- to support the part of the presser foot which would otherwise slant up or down. Without this aid one can easily skip stitches or break needles. These lifts can be purchased at sewing machine shops.

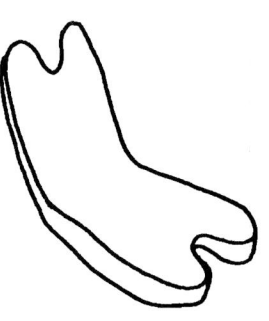

The lined rainjacket shown was made from Vogue 2461. The red Ultra Leather® jacket was Burda 7200. The green Ultra Suede® raincoat was Vogue 9724, now discontinued but Vogue 2625 is very similar if cut about 12" - 14" longer. Patterns come and go in availability but close substitutions can frequently be found with a little research.

Program 4: Sweatering

What works in your mind may, in reality, turn out to be an absolute bomb. Such was the case with an extremely thick cotton sweatering shown at the opening of this program. Meant to be a coat-like sweater with a fur collar to be added, the sweater bodies stretched enormously. All the seams were therefore stabilized with strips of Ultra Suede®, topstitched to both decorate and prevent stretch. The suede nicely accomplished both but to no avail. The interior of each sweater part still stretched so ridiculously that it would have wrapped you and me and your Aunt Mary with a little room to spare! This was not working.

Think of the alternatives. A reasonable one would be to fuse an interfacing to the entire inside to stop the expansion. Then that would need to be lined to cover up the utilitarian interfacing. The whole project already weighed a ton and it was growing up to be an uglier prospect with each passing moment. There are times when it simply is not worth wasting any more time on a lost cause. Admit defeat and throw it out if there is no way to transform the vision to reality.

Was it an absolute waste? No. Turned out a friend loved it, and it was gladly given to her. More importantly it was a real learning experience, for the next time I will consider weight and stretch and bulky thickness very carefully before I foolishly buy it! Maybe there are no bad fabrics but there are certainly personal preferences which need to be sorted out and defined to promote satisfaction.

There are about three ways to buy sweater fabric. One is sweatering by the yard. This is a long knit fabric rolled on a bolt, maybe flat, maybe tubular knit. You simply have cut off as much yardage as you request. This has no finished edges, no ribbed bottoms, so finishings must be added.

A second way to buy sweatering is in sweater bodies. These are tubular knit pieces with finished ribbed bottoms. If these are purchased singly remember they may be knit in many different sizes and must be measured to be sure one piece is large enough for your body with whatever amount of extra ease you prefer. Another piece is needed, the two seamed at the sides, if one is not roomy enough. Others of these pieces with finished ribbing at the bottom are flat knit but work in the same way. A second piece is then utilized for cutting the two sleeves. Even though lower edges are finished, a ribbing, a facing, a binding or perhaps a collar will be needed to finish the neck edge.

The third way to buy sweatering is in a kit which has enough fabric, probably bottoms finished by ribbing, to provide the body, the sleeves, separate neck ribbing, and possibly a large extra piece for a skirt. Here again, be sure of ample sizing on all pieces before purchasing and cutting. This is an all-inclusive unit with no extra purchases needed.

Any of these are cut out with a pattern of your choice and the cutting surface may be your first consideration. If you are a "rug cutter" be careful. The texture of the carpeting as you smooth the sweatering out on it may hold your fabric in a stretched out position. A smooth surface might be more appropriate to allow the knit fabric to relax.

Once cut out, curling edges are a problem in some. If so, glue stick these edges right sides together and allow to dry before sewing or serging. On the sewing machine it would be a good idea to use some sort of a horizontal stitch pattern both to give the seams a little stretch, and also for a more finished appearance.

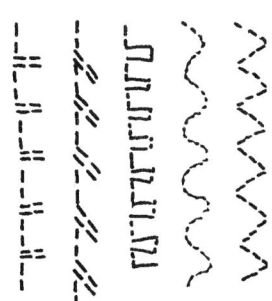

Here are some possibilities you might find among your stitch selections. -sketch 4.1-

Trim off extra fabric close to stitching.

If serger joining is your preference use 4 threads to best cut, join, finish all in one operation. If you have an overlock with a differential feed, you'll love it in sewing sweaters to eliminate the rippled edges. For those in the market for a new serger, this is a great feature. It means that the presser foot and lower feed work in such a way as to compress the fabric being stitched and no ripples result on the edges.

Sometimes seams need to be stabilized whether sewing on sewing machine or on a serger. Staytape, seam tape, thin narrow selvage strips, twill tape all work well to eliminate stretching seams. This is most often used on horizontal seams, especially those ribbed knits that really give, than on vertical seams.

Even though most sweater seams are sewn together and trimmed down to the thread finish, some of the very thin knits used in sweater dresses are treated differently. Because they are so thin and these usual techniques would show a bulky impression on the outside, it might be better to first finish the seam edges, then merely machine stitch a plain 5/8" seam and press it open for the best exterior appearance. Try various techniques on your scraps to find the best way before sewing the garment itself.

The hems on these same dress knits must be carefully considered. Suggestions that work well depending on individual fabric characteristics are: -sketch 4.2-

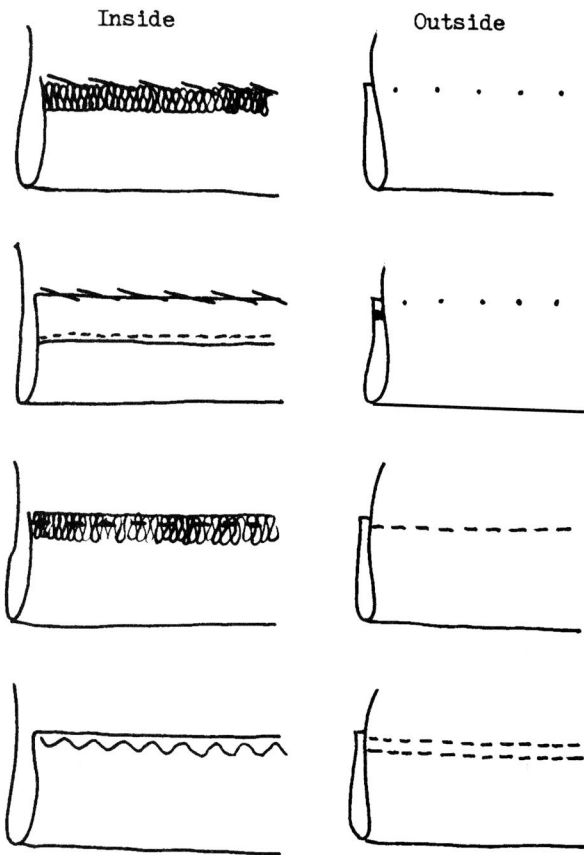

Serge raw edge and hem by hand

Use hem tape and hem by hand

Serge, turn up hem, machine topstitch

Turn up hem, double needle topstitch, trim excess fabric

These dress knits often need a zipper closing. If there is topstitching elsewhere it is probably best to topstitch the zipper also.

-sketch 4.3- Dress back with machine stitched zipper and other topstitching.

If on the other hand, a dress has no other stitching that shows, it is better to use an invisible zipper where only the tab shows, or hand pick the zipper in place. -sketch 4.4-

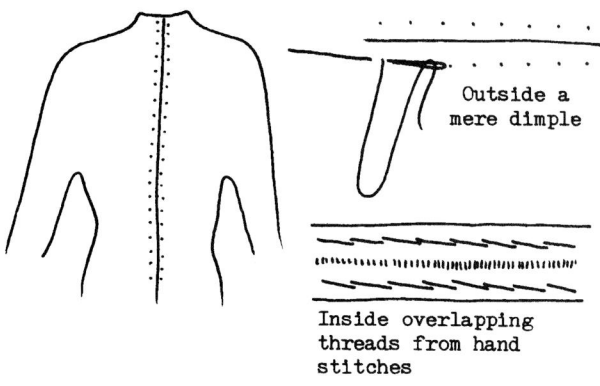

Only slight dimples show on the outside with hand picking. This is done from the outside and is actually a slight backstitch at each stroke.

Also with these thin sweater knit dresses, think stretch and recovery. Before construction check to be sure when stretched out sideways, the fabric will recover to its original size. If it does not you are being warned that it will quickly look baggy and seat sprung. To prevent this, underline (staystitch a lining fabric of the same pattern cut, to the knit wrong side) before constructing seams. An underlining is also nice to hem to so that no stitches will show on the outside of the garment.

These necklines will either have turtle neck type collars, facings on jewel necks or binding on edges in all probability. They would all be treated as any other fabrics.

Heavier sweater knits usually have ribbing at neck and wrists. If this is of the same sweater fabric, make sure the stretch recovers completely so that it always goes snugly back into place. If it does not it may be necessary to pair it with a harmonizing or contrasting rib knit which does recover in size. These ribbings are usually used in ratios of 2:3 or 3:4 depending on how great their stretch. This means 20 inches of rib will be stitched to 30 inches of garment edge or 30 inches of rib will be attached to 40 inches of sweater lower edge. It would be wise in making the decision of how big, to fold over the anticipated amount, pin and actually slide over your head, wrist or hips to see if it works as planned. Adjust accordingly before cutting off.

As in sketch 4.5 stitch the joining in a small seam and open up the seam allowances to distribute the bulk.

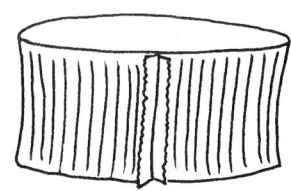

Fold this in half, wrong sides together, and mark each quarter with a pin. -Sketch 4.6- Also pin-mark the quarter points of the garment edge the ribbing will join.

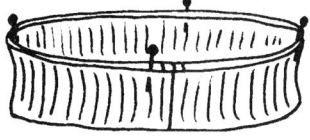

Garment wrong side out, pin the two raw edges of the ribbing to the right side of the garment edge, as in sketch 4.7, matching quarter points. Stretching the ribbings as you progress, stitch or serge the edges together removing pins just before you reach them.

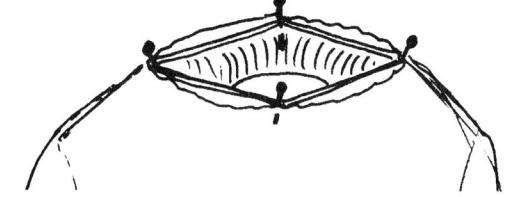

If this is a cardigan sweater the front opening and back neck edge can be finished with self ribbing cut lengthwise rather than crosswise, any woven or knit fabric to contrast, Ultra Suede® foldover trim, grosgrain ribbon on the underside, or any finish which seems appropriate. Be sure the garment front edge is neither stretched out nor condensed smaller when the band is being applied. If buttonholes will be stitched, a little patch of fusible interfacing might be needed to stabilize stretchy ribbings.

The burgundy sweater knit dress was Vogue 7914. The aqua two piece dress was Vogue 9104. The oversize purple cardigan was Burda 5859. Pink and black sweater worn Great Copy Patterns 107. Pink liquid leather pants worn Great Copy Patterns 610.

Program 5: One Layer Coat

Making a one layer coat is a quick, easy project and suitable for all skill levels. This is a great transitional coat when you need something ... but it's not cold enough for a heavy coat with all its many layers. This is also unbeatable for travel. It might even take the shape of a fitted little Austrian boiled wool jacket. Or perhaps it goes casual in a short fun coat to wear with pants.

One layer means you see both sides, so the fabric must be attractive either way. In fact, you can plan a reversible if you like. This fabric can be a woven mohair or wool for a warm but relatively weightless coat. There are some knits which would also be terrific ... fleece type which are washable as an added bonus.

The pattern should be something very simple and with a loose fit unless the fabric is very sturdy and stable to hold its shape. Every pattern brand will have several appropriate choices. It may have buttons and pockets or not, worn loose or belted. You're the designer and make the choices.

Remove the pattern from the envelope but only the main pieces ... front, back, sleeve, collar and pocket will be used. All the rest can be put back in the envelope. Trim off extra paper and pin together to try on, or else compare your measurements with those of the pattern to determine if alterations will be needed. Check intended hem width because you will probably use less and might save some fabric in cutting.

Of the coats shown, one was made from a coat pattern, the other two were variations of a T shirt pattern. Be sure to lay the pieces all in the same direction as most fabrics you would use for this would have a nap. Naps go in the down direction for longer wear maintaining a newer look. If the nap goes up there is a greater tendency to pill, rough up, and take on a much worn look. The choice of directions is yours.

The grey mohair coat with the cozy collar was shown and explained in the series I book but briefly, this is how you lay a T shirt pattern (they are all similar so any brand will do) to make a coat. Sketch 5.1 shows the T shirt back and front on the fabric. The dotted lines are the original pattern. The solid lines are the cutting lines as the sleeves are cut long, the side seams a little wider, the length as much longer as you want. Add an opening in front with an overlap. This easily it can actually be done. The pockets are cut about the size of this book page with 2 rounded off corners. The collar is cut on the fold and is almost a rectangle about 8" high and the lower line measures the same as the front and back neckline.

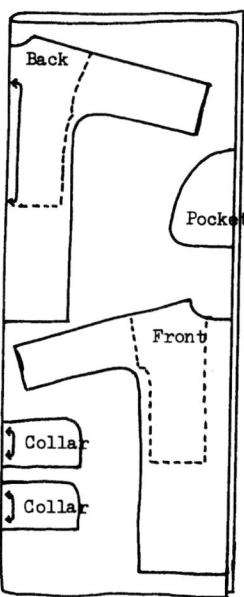

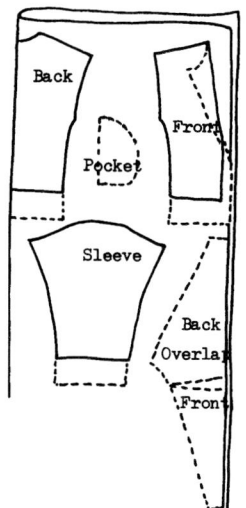

The turquoise polar fleece fun coat with the fringed collar was cut with the same T shirt pattern and its layout is sketch 5.2.

The back is cut same as T shirt adding 4"-6" in length. The front needs the same length added and the center front edge is folded over from shoulder point to waist so it is a deep V neck. The sleeve pattern is folded in half lengthwise and cut on the fold, one sleeve above the other. The pattern front and back are then overlapped at their shoulder stitching lines tapering to 1" more overlap out at the sleeve edge. Place this overlapped shoulder line perpendicular to the fabric selvages. Again fold back the center front edge from shoulder point to waist to cut a deep V neck. Add a seam allowance to the center back edge. Cut the collar layers from center front waist, out as wide as possible at shoulder, taper narrower at center back waist. Cut two pocket layers wherever they will fit approximately the size of this page with corners rounded on one side.

The construction of the two T shirt coats is similar. On the jacket front side seam,
1. slightly below the waistline and again 7" below that, clip into the seam allowance, press the seam under, topstitch it in place. -sketch 5.3- Position a pocket layer under it, pin in place, topstitch around the pocket edge to permanently hold it in place. If this fabric will fray, press under a seam allowance first before attaching the pocket to the coat front, referring to sketch 5.3.

2. Stitch the shoulder seams of coat back and front together, finishing as you prefer (suggestions later). Stitch the center back collar seam together and finish on the pant coat. The long coat was cut on the fold.

3. Pin the right side of collar neck edge to the wrong side of coat neck and stitch. Press seam toward coat after grading the seam edges, shortest one between layers. Finish.

4. Stitch sleeve in armscye, finish. Stitch underarm-side seams.

The seam choices are infinite, but here are a few suggestions:

Serge: The whole garment could be constructed and finished in one operation on a 4-thread serger. Press seams to one side and be done with it, or topstitch them in place after overlocking. From the outside this gives the appearance of a flat felled seam. -sketch 5.4-

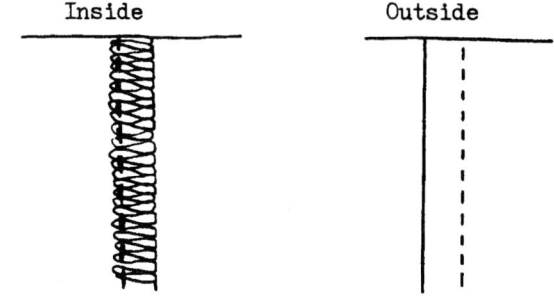

Flat Felled: The traditional flat felled seam begins like a plain 5/8" seam. Press it open, trim one side down smaller than 1/4". Press the long seam over it, press under a little hem on its edge. Edge stitch along that fold. -sketch 5.5-

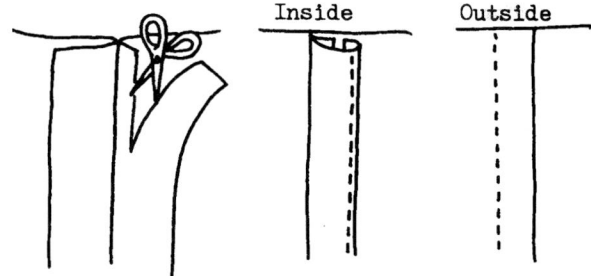

If the fabric is not ravelly (as in a knit fleece or boiled wool) the second turn under is unnecessary. Instead trim off a little of that long edge and stitch the raw edge down. The exterior appearance will be the same but you will eliminate some bulk.

Moss Fringe: This is a good idea for a real ravelly fabric. Stitch a 5/8" seam wrong sides together so that the seam allowances are on the outside. Press them to one side and topstitch them down 1/8" from the original seam. Fray out all the fabric yarns up to your stitching lines. This is pretty in mohair. -sketch 5.6-

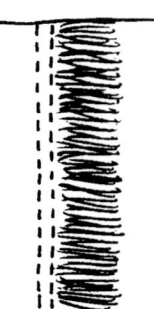

Couched Yarns: When the above seam is pressed to one side, rather than ravelling to the stitching line, just fray a few yarns off the edge. Loosely twist these into a cord and place it over the raw edges. Attach it down to the coat while securing the seam in place by machine stitching with a zigzag or a blind hem stitch. -sketch 5.7- In either case the stitching blends in and doesn't show, but it provides a pretty trim.

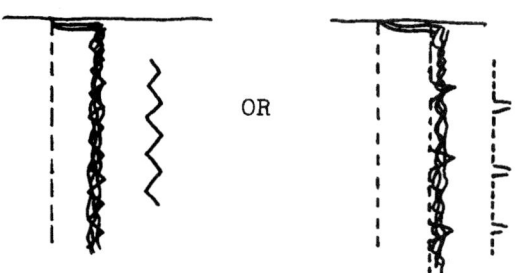

Suede Trim: Press open a 5/8" seam stitched to the outside. Trim both seam allowances off to less than 1/4". Topstitch over this a 1/2" strip of Ultra Suede® cut with pinking shears or with straight scissors. -sketch 5.8-

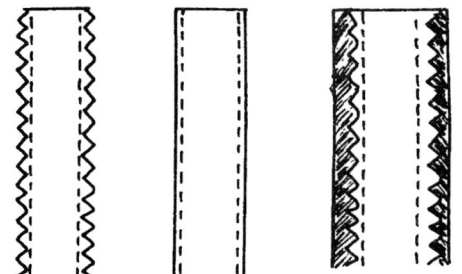

BUTTONHOLES present another challenge as with only one layer of fabric, reinforcement must be provided. Some ideas for these:

Ultra Suede®: Fuse a rectangle on the front side of the coat which is 1/4" larger on all sides than the buttonholes will be. Fuse to the coat underside another suede patch 1/16" larger all around than the first, to be sure they will both be caught in the stitching. Slash with a craft knife down the center and stitch around it. -sketch 5.9-

A suede variation would be to fuse a suede patch on the underside only to reinforce. On the top make a standard machine buttonhole. -sketch 5.10-

Twisted Cord: A few yarns frayed from the fabric can be nicely twisted on the bobbin winder of your machine. Thread 3 or 4 of these yarns together through the bobbin hole letting them extend about one inch beyond. Clamp the bobbin on the winder and hold out straight the other ends of the yarn. Push the power pedal and the yarns will twist so tightly that eventually they will begin to shorten and pull in. -sketch 5.11- Stop the power.

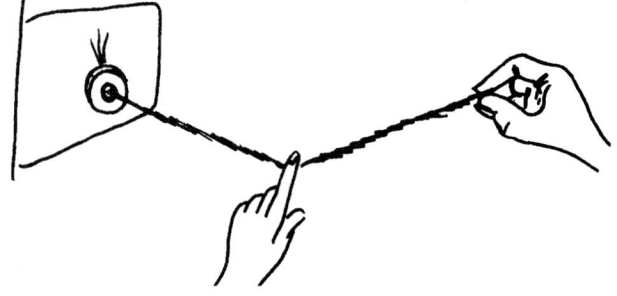

It will back twist when you put a finger in the center and let your other hand release the tension, doubling the yarn ply. This makes a really nice matching button loop or several, bartacked between each to hold in place.
-sketch 5.12-

The burgundy coat pattern is Simplicity 9860.

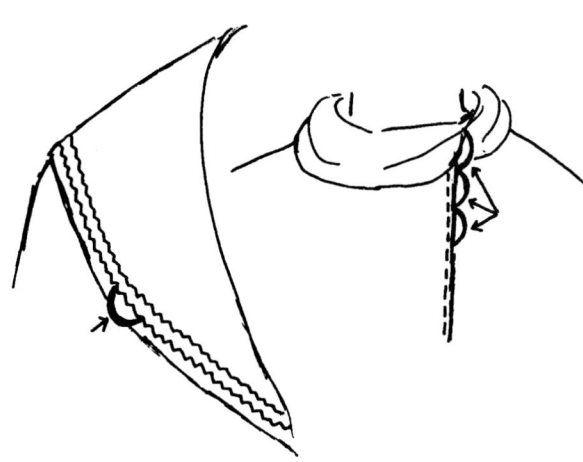

Program 6: On The Edge

The one layer coat continues and after you've made decisions on seams, pockets, buttonholes or any other interior construction detail ... what kind of a finish would you like to have ON THE EDGE?

Of the coats shown, here is an idea borrowed from one of the nation's pricey retailers. When the fabric will not fray, edges need not be securely stitched. The pant coat therefore was finished in a very casual, fun technique. The knit polar fleece was fringed all around the outer edge of the really large collar in the easiest way imaginable ... with scissors! Every 1/4", a 3" slash was made being careful to cut these very straight and uniformly. - sketch 6.1 -

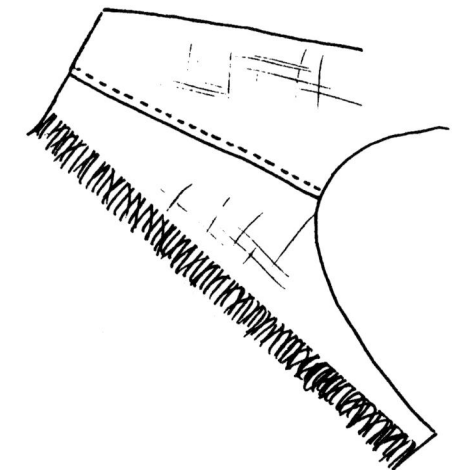

Sketch 6.2

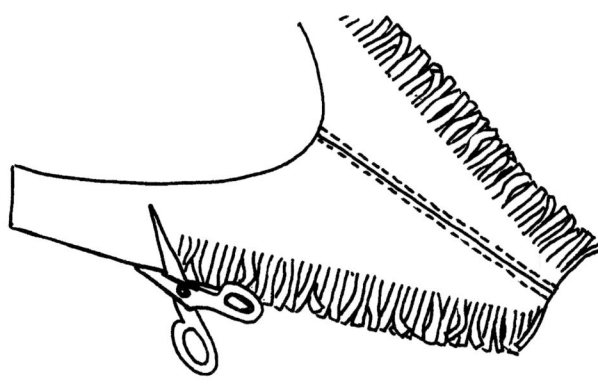

The lower hem could also be slashed in this same way. Because of the knit construction these pieces will not pull off even with repeated washings. This could also work on some woven fabrics which are so heavily felted that they won't fray. The sleeve is hemmed by turning the edge up once and topstitching. The center front edges below the collar are also turned once and stitched.

Had that same coat been made out of a ravely fabric it would have been pretty to fringe the edges to that same 3" depth just as one would on the edges of a shawl.
-sketch 6.2-

The finished jacket is shown in sketch 6.3 and is photographed elsewhere in the book in a turquoise color.

The grey mohair coat, made from a T shirt pattern also, was edge finished by fold-

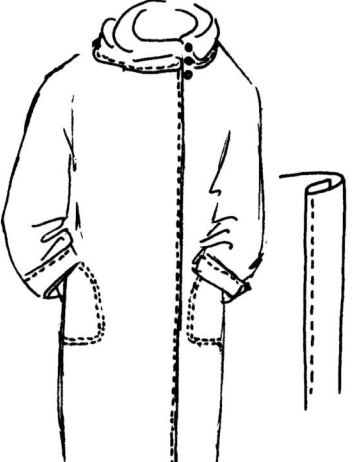

ing the fabric twice to the underside, steam pressing it all carefully and topstitching to hold it in place. Sketch 6.4 shows this. These are both coats to make in a short part of a day, easy enough for a beginning sewer. Even a very experienced sewer however, will find these fun, very wearable, and useful in the wardrobe.

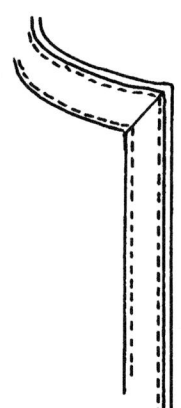
On the Austrian influenced boiled wool jackets and vests, ravelling is not a problem for these fabrics, either knit or woven. Closely felted fabric edges are rather secure. Traditionally they are bound with foldover braid but it is also possible to simply topstitch some ribbon along the raw edge, not enclosing it. -sketch 6.5-

These jackets and vests would be the perfect candidates for edging with some of the wonderful decorative stitches your machine will do. Some of my favorites which I have found to work will are shown in sketch 6.6. After the stitching is done near the fabric edge, the little excess fabric is cut off.

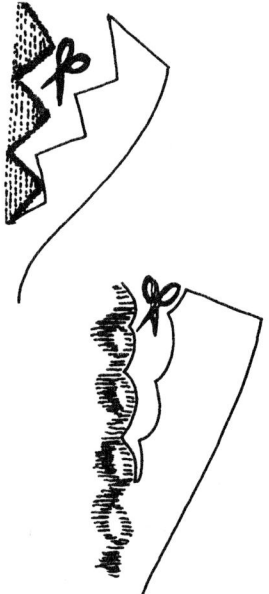

Some extra presser foot attachments your sewing machine dealer can supply will unearth a lot of other possibilities. Sketch 6.7 shows a 7-hole foot which securely holds seven strands of perle cotton or other cord in place straightening out the cords as you proceed. Used in combination with some decorative stitch which holds all these cords in place, you can produce a beautiful edge with your choice of color combination. It simulates a decorative braid.

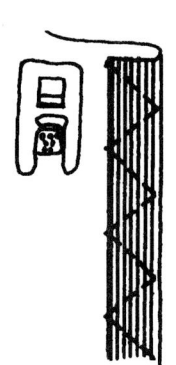

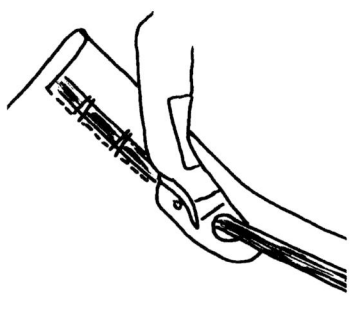
A wide braiding foot, sketch 6.8, allows you to use a multitude of cords made commercially to cover the raw edge of the fabric after it has been folded back. This foot will even permit pearls by the yard to go through its opening while it holds the strand securely in place. It can be attached by a zigzag stitch or perhaps a blind hem stitch as shown.

Folding the edge to the garment outside in this manner is also good when covering with decorative ribbons or narrow strips of Ultra Suede®. There are two ways to do this. One is a two-step process where on the wrong side of the fabric you would lap the ribbon or suede half on, half off the fabric edge. -sketch 6.9- Edge stitch in place. Fold over the edge to the right side and edge stitch the other trim edge, securing everything flat to the main body of the garment.

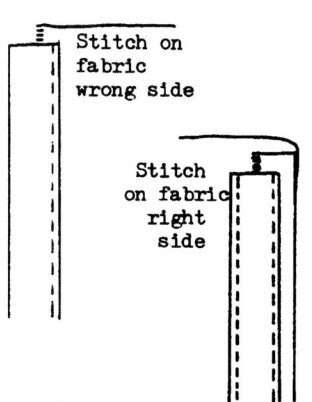

Because the burgundy coat on the program was a rather thick, spongy fabric even though it was weightless, I chose to use a one-step stitching. -sketch 6.10- The edge 5/8" seam allowance was first pressed to the right side, then that edge covered with the suede stripe and both trim edges stitched.

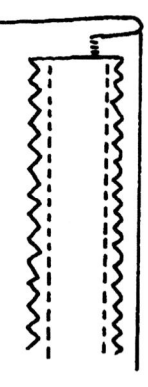

The suede strips can be cut with pinking shears, straight edge shears, or a rotary cutter. These two rows of stitching held the edges firmer and flatter which seemed appropriate for the fabric. Because the large collar is cut in one with the coat, both coat and collar would not have the trim on top. -sketch 6.11- My choice was to have it on the collar, so below the breakpoint only stitching lines show on the coat outside. The suede strip below that point is on the inside of the coat.

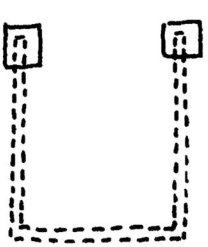

Because this coat has patch pockets, there are little suede patches fused to the inside of the coat at the two top pocket corners, the stress points. -sketch 6.12-

Those little suede patches are also used under the buttons to reinforce and put all the stress on the suede, not on the one layer of loosely woven fabric.

Instead of folding over the raw edge of the coat it could be left raw in a single layer. After the suede trim is edge stitched on both edges, fray yarns out of the easily ravelled fabric up to the stitching line. -sketch 6.13-

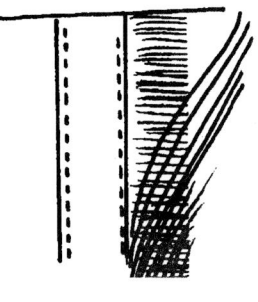

Another thought is to eliminate the suede strip and instead press a 1" strip of the self fabric almost in half but with the top layer shorter. -sketch 6.14- Stitch its fold 5/8" from the fabric edge, then ravel out all three layers for a thick moss fringe.

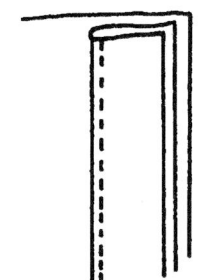 

With the edge out straight several other coverings are possible. Fold over braid can be purchased by the yard to sew on in one step, especially if the underside is longer so that you'll be sure to catch both layers. This may be straight stitched in place or, if the thread is a perfect color match, zigzag may anchor both layers more firmly. -sketch 6.15-

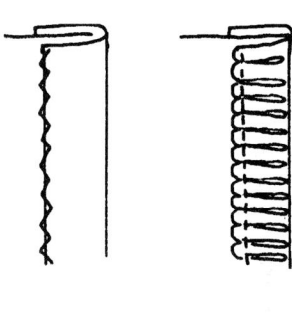

Instead of a commercial braid, Ultra Suede® strips may be used. Cut these about 1" wide. To then press this in half is most difficult as it must be covered by a press cloth. This would mean pressing accuracy is unlikely. The easy way is to edge stitch a fold rather than pressing, making sure as you proceed that the under layer is slightly wider. -sketch 6.16- Sandwich this over the raw edge, longer layer underneath, and edge stitch the three layers together.

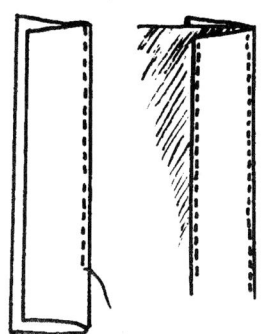

Or cut this suede 1 1/2" wide. Using a scallop stitch, or something similar which your machine can do, stitch the fold rather than using a straight stitch. -sketch 6.17- Trim the suede fold off close to the scallop stitching. Sandwich over fabric edge and edgestitch all together. It is also possible, if you find it easier, to first press a fusible release sheet to the suede wrong side so that when it is sandwiched over the fabric, it can be fused before stitching. Another idea is to insert a thin strip of fusible web under the suede edge and fusing after the fabric has been positioned between layers.

Your serger can do some nice edge finishing also. Try flatlocking the edge with ribbon floss, perle cotton, candlelight, or any of the lovely novelty threads. They produce attractive, decorative edges which are very sturdy and serviceable. The decorative thread is used in the upper looper only and its tension is set at the lowest. The left needle and the lower looper are threaded with regular thread and both their tensions are tightened. -sketch 6.18-

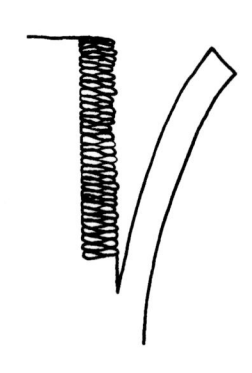

You'll find a quick, easy one-layer coat a very valuable addition to your wardrobe.

The Austrian boiled wool jackets and vests courtesy of Sue Hausmann, education director for Viking Sewing Machines.

Program 4

Program 10

Program 11

Sewing Conn

Program 2

Program 3

Program 5

Program 7

My better half, Jo
Upstairs is Andy, g

Program 8

-tion III Ideas

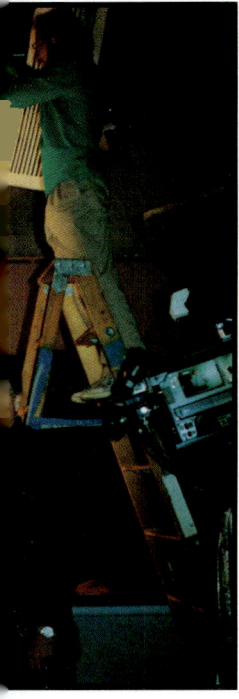

o the business half.
n lights and camera.

Program 8

Program 10

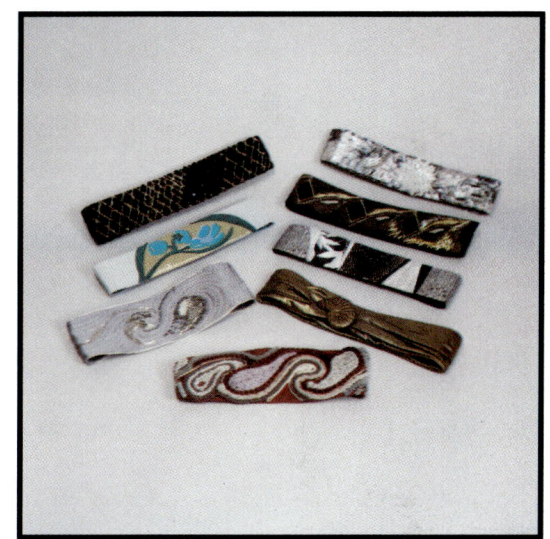

Program 12

Program 13

Program 2

Program 8

Program 7: Altering Ultra Suede® Garments

Some sewers are still afraid to work with the manmade suedes for a couple of reasons. Considering the cost of the fabric,

1. What if the style of the garment goes out of fashion?

The answer to this is simple. Make the suede garment or any expensive fabric into a classic style which will be fashionable indefinitely. A future series program will deal in restyling Ultra Suede® however.

2. What if I gain weight?

This we'll deal with now so you realize changing size is entirely possible with pleasant results.

That very thing happened to me. A suit which was my own original design became too tight in the upper skirt area. Much to my dismay I had gained 2 inches rendering the skirt unwearable.

First remove the waistband and release the lining. It is a good idea to always line suede garments as they move more easily with the slippery layer, feel more comfortable and luxurious. This skirt has frontier pockets.

-sketch 7.1- A lucky bonus was, in making this skirt originally, the use of suede for the entire pocket layer closer to my body -labeled A- instead of only using suede where it showed plus lining fabric inside. There was also a zipper inside this pocket. Remove that completely to be put somewhere else, a problem we'll solve in a little while. Remove stitching around inner edges of frontier pockets as shown in sketch 7.2, separating the suede and lining layers.

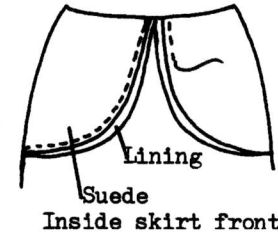

With all this area loose, try on the skirt and adjust the pocket areas, moving the side fronts outward from the center panel. Pin in place at waist.
-sketch 7.3-

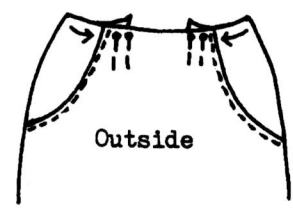

Staystitch adjusted layers together at waist. On a flat surface pin together the inner edges of pocket layers as they want to position themselves. Stitch the inner curved line connecting the two pocket layers. Trim off the excess lining layer which is the darkened parts of sketch 7.4. This is a really easy sure cure with nothing left to do but adding a zipper to the skirt back and putting on a new or an extended waistband. It is not always so lucky as to have the frontier pockets! Other alteration possibilities exist.

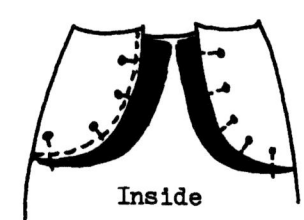

The suede construction is probably one of two methods:
1. conventional seams,
2. lapped seams.

Either of these type seams can be let out.

Conventional seams are simply the same 5/8" seam one would stitch on every fabric, then press open. -sketch 7.5- Carefully remove the stitching from this and it is likely the stitching lines will show. Obscure them as much as possible by just running a fingernail back and forth over it to rough up the nap making the obvious needle holes less noticeable. With an iron or press, a presscloth on top of the

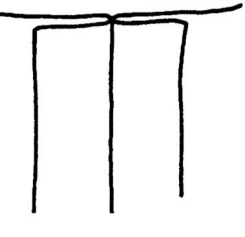

suede and plenty of steam, press the seam edges to flatten and restore the new look.

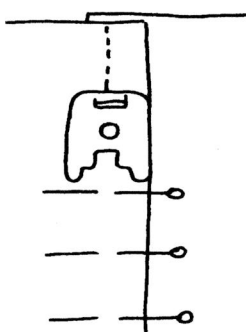

Then overlap front over back seam 3/8" to 5/8" ... depending on how much excess you must gain at each seam ... and pin in place.
-sketch 7.6-

Using a small (#70 - 80) stretch needle, stitch length 6 - 8 per inch, stitch one line of topstitching through the layers 1/4" away from the suede edge. Using the presser foot edge as a guide is the easiest way to get a straight line.

Stitch a second row of edge stitching very close to the suede edge. Some gradation or mark on your presser foot will hopefully allow this capability so you can again gauge a straight line.
-sketch 7.7- You have just created a lapped seam.

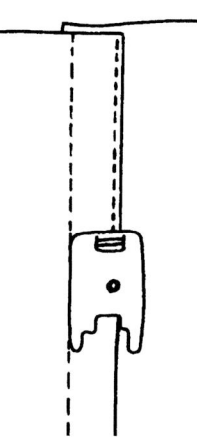

If you already had these lapped seams on your garment, there will be less suede hidden in the seams for expansion use. Some letting out is still possible, however.

Remove the stitching and rough up the suede same as before to obscure old stitches. Steam press flat. Cut a 1" strip of the same suede if you are so lucky as to have a piece left over. If not, any similar color or even one which is completely different will work, as this will be underneath and not actually show. Fuse a strip of a fusible release sheet to the strip of suede.

Wrong sides of the garment up, butt the two edges together. Position the suede strip over the joining, fusible side down. Using a presscloth and steam, fuse the strip to the garment.
-sketch 7.8-

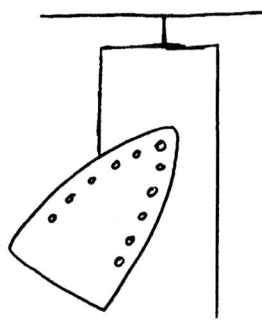

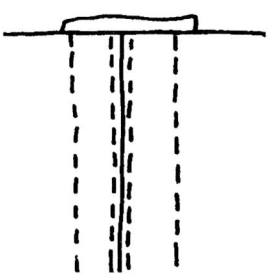

From the right side, edge stitch and topstitch both sides of the joining. If any of the old lines show, run more stitching lines to mask them. -sketch 7.9-

If still more growth is needed than can be found in letting out seams, add panels. The same color would be marvelous. If this is impossible, think colorblocking. Could an extra panel be added on a jacket to both the under sleeve and the side front? -sketch 7.10- Or slash the whole front and back and add a stripe of suede or even another fabric? Sweatering? Quilting?
-sketch 7.11-

 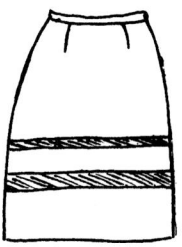 

Perhaps a panel of suede, so it doesn't look colorblocked or let-out, could have its edges blended. This is a great fashion period for lots of embellishment, so think what you can do getting very creative.

Create an opening somewhere, maybe by opening a seam or maybe by cutting a new opening. Position on the board a new strip of suede cut as wide as the expansion width needed plus two inches. Overlap the two garment edges by 1" on each side of the wide strip. Fuse a tiny ribbon of fusible web between layers as indicated in sketch 7.12 where the dotted lines appear.

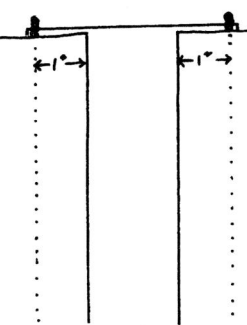

Cut long slashes into the loose suede on each side of the opening. -sketch 7.13-

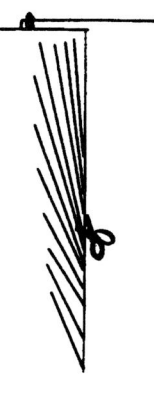

Beginning with the outer slashed strip, machine stitch it down while curving it as you proceed. Stitch out to the first point, needle in down position, lift foot, pivot, foot down stitch back up the other side to its origin. Repeat this on all strips until every one is stitched, blending into the new inset. -sketch 7.14 and 7.15-

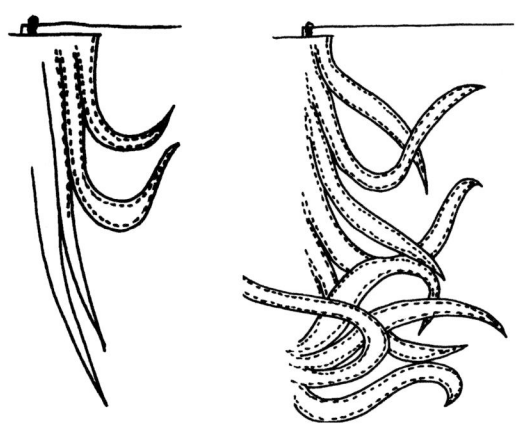

This is wonderful fun and much easier than it looks.

If you have a more geometric spirit consider some straighter lines as in figure 7.16 to blend two colors together, trimming off extra strips of the original suede to blend in the new addition. These strips of varying sizes are probably fused in place, then later stitched.

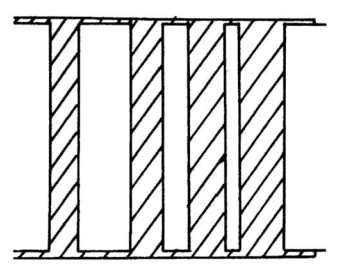

Are the wheels spinning in your head coming up with other ideas? The possibilities are limitless.

To add a zipper in suede where there isn't a seam -sketch 7.17- (next page):

1. Draw a straight line where the zipper will be, measuring the desired length, and cut a slash.

2. From the backside, fuse a reinforcement piece of suede cut 1" wide and 1" longer than opening.

3. Stitch around the opening, 1/8" away from cut edge.

4. Glue stick zipper to underside, carefully centering it, right side against suede reinforcement. If this zipper is purchased 2" longer than desired length, the problem of stitching around the tab is eliminated. The extra length, tab zipped to top, would be up and above the garment.

5. With a 1/2" wide strip of scotch tape on top to use as a straight line gauge, stitch at its edge sewing the zipper to the skirt.

6. Carefully, with small sharp-pointed scissors, cut down the under layer opening using the upper layer opening as a guide. The description of this sounds much more diffi-

Sketch 7.17

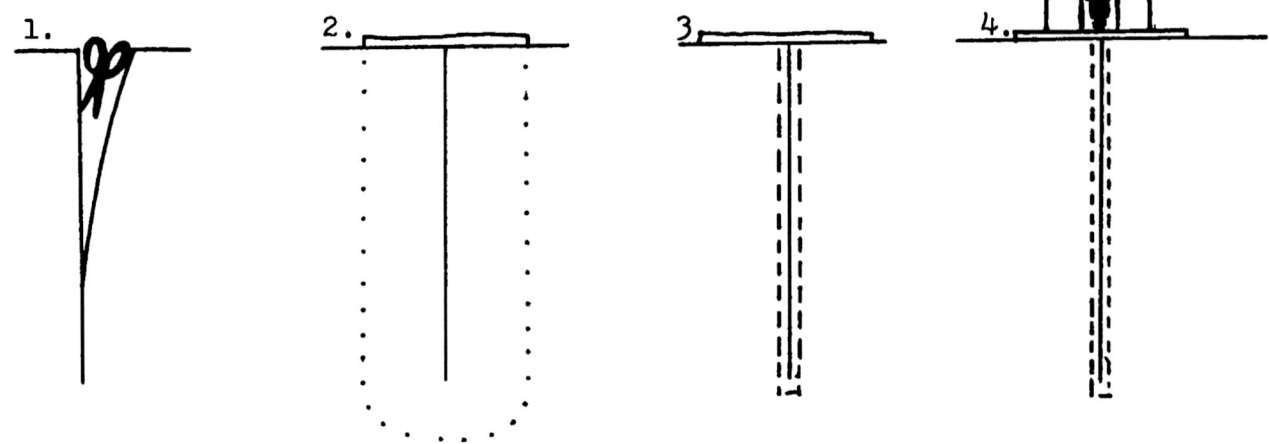

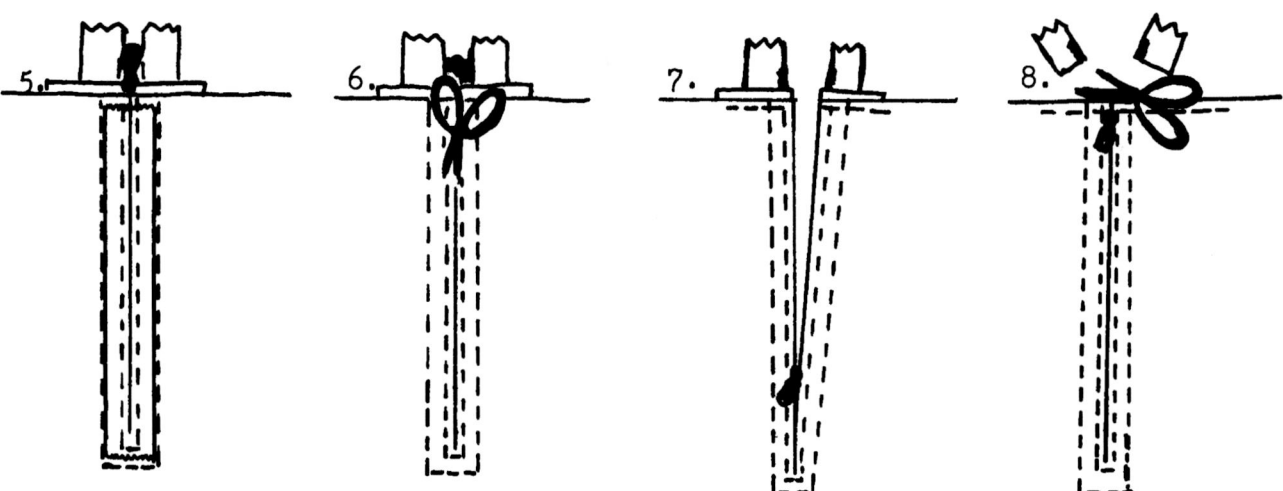

cult than the job actually will be. The zipper is still zipped to this point.

7. Unzip the zipper and with the tab down in the garment area, staystitch across the top of the two zipper tapes to the suedes and backstitch. This provides a stopper so the tab cannot accidently be zipped off the unprotected upper ends.

8. Trim off the upper zipper ends, apply waistband.

Program 8: Distorting the Facts

A viewer wrote to say she likes the idea of appliqueing on clothing or other items ... but hers always came out looking very childlike ... and that wasn't her intent. Fact of the matter is ... appliques are just great on children's clothing or in children's rooms. But to add a little sophistication to a simple theme ... distort the facts.

But the viewer wanted a more sophisticated look. Any non-artist can accomplish this by distorting the facts. Begin by simplifying the fish idea. Reduce the outline to the simplest lines possible as in sketch 8.2 which can be traced on the rough side of a fusible release sheet (Wonder Under® is an example of one available). Fuse this to some fabric or some manmade suede. Peel off the paper.

For example, a little fanciful fish like sketch 8.1 can be appliqued to a child's T shirt. Add a wiggly eye or a button eye (sewn on very securely). With decorative machine stitching embroider some hearts for air bubbles, scallops for waves and we have a terrific picture for children's clothing or room decor.

Cut out the fish pieces and arrange them, fusible side down, spreading them out with space between each piece, on a sweater, T shirt or whatever garment seems appropriate.-sketch 8.3- When positioned to your satisfaction, cover with a press cloth and fuse with an iron or on a press.

Sketch 8.2

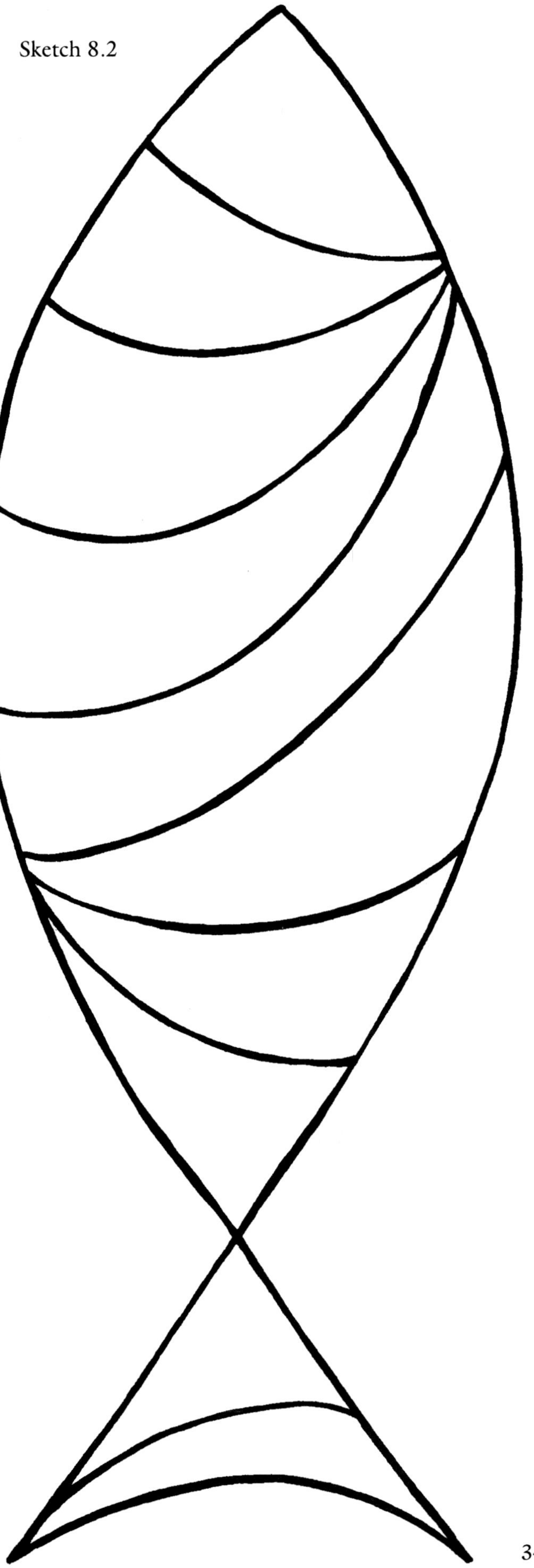

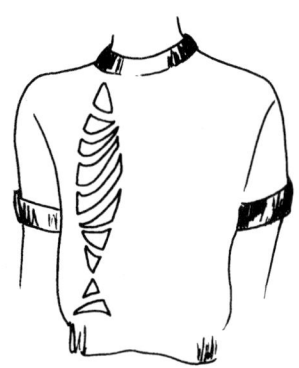

When cool, stitch around each piece for permanency. If you used a suede, straight stitching will be suitable. If a woven or knit fabric, satin stitch all edges so nothing will fray in the wash.

Simplifying then distorting the fact that this was a fish added some sophistication to this design. Sometimes the color combination will add sophistication if it is mainly neutrals, for example. Or the opposite extreme, really bright but discordant colors to jar your sensibilities a little might work nicely.

Sketch 8.4

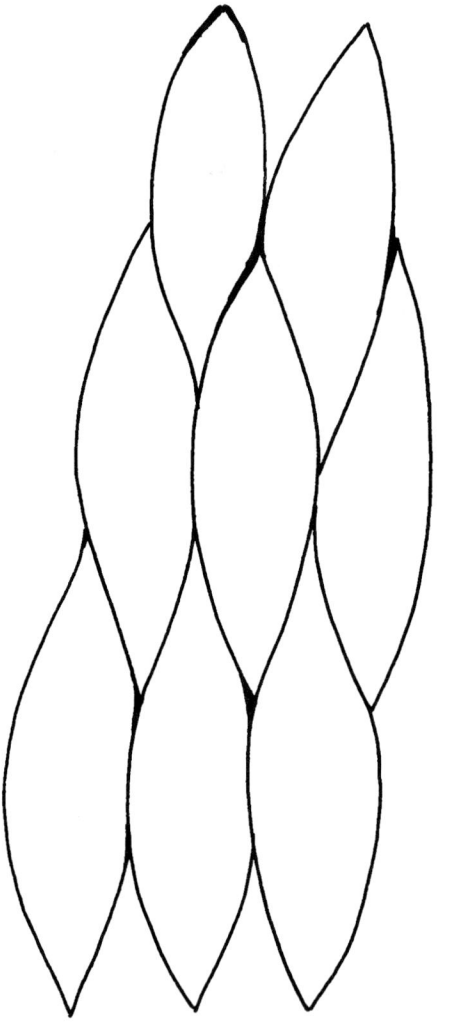

Picture for example, willow branches done in red-orange, red, magenta, and purple. Trace sketch 8.4 on the rough side of fusible release sheets four times. Each of these four sheets can then be fused to the back side of four different fabrics. I used four pieces of Ultra Suede® in the colors mentioned above.

To set a design, cut two pieces of yarn or thick cord 18" long. Couch these on a sweater front for one, down the sleeve for the other. Couching is zigzag stitching over the cord to attach it to the garment. As you stitch, gently curve the yarn back and forth into a slight S curve. -sketch 8.5-

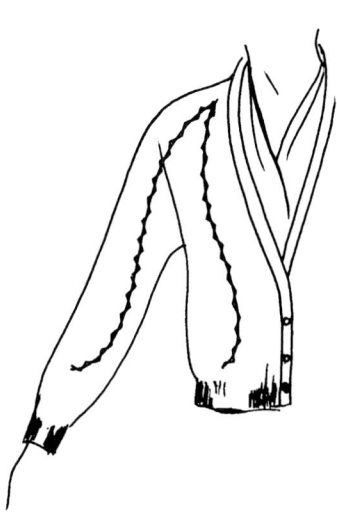

Peel the release sheet from your fused leaves and the outline of each will remain on the fabric. Cut the leaves apart on the lines and position them all along one side of a yarn "branch", fusible side down. Cover with a press cloth and fuse. When cool, straight stitch a "vein" down the center of each to keep permanently anchored. If you used a ravelly fabric, it would be a good idea to satin stitch the outer edge of each. -sketch 8.6-

Using the same color but a contrast of textures is another way to do an applique. Simple tulip shapes for example are quite interesting when used in a shiny fabric on a dull background. -sketch 8.7- A different twist to the same idea would be using a napped fabric and cutting the tulips from the same fabric but with the nap running the opposite direction. The play of light on this

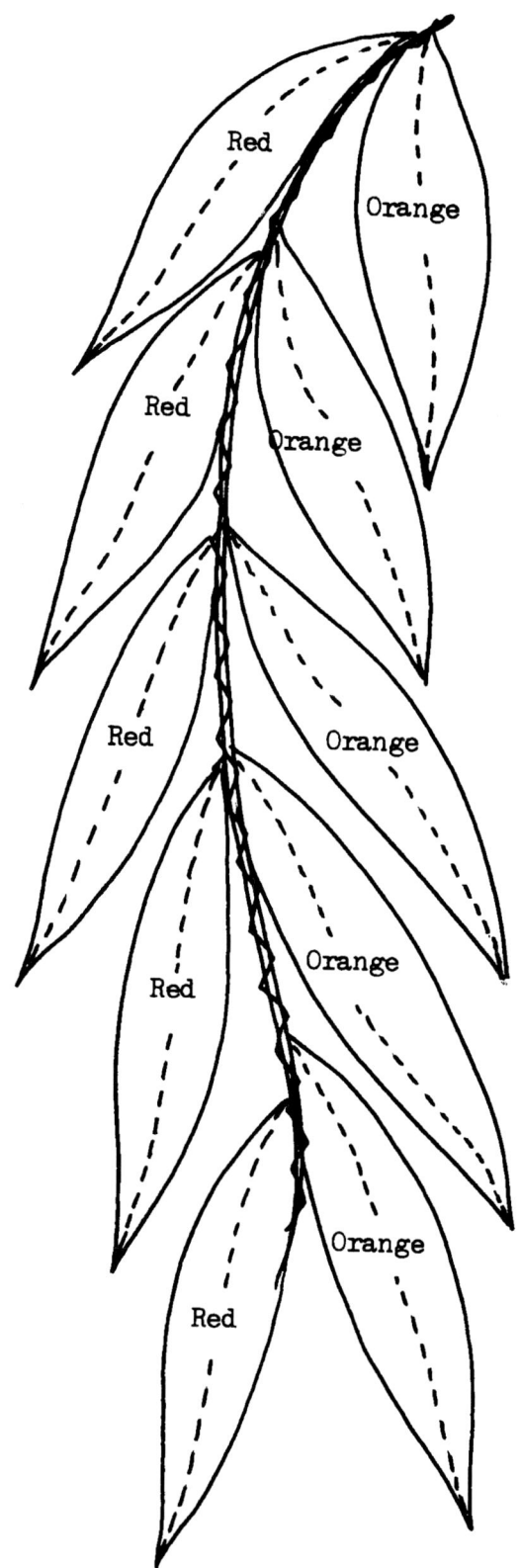

Sketch 8.6

makes the background look dark with light tulips on it ... or the reverse depending on the nap directions.

Sketch 8.7

Sketch 8.8

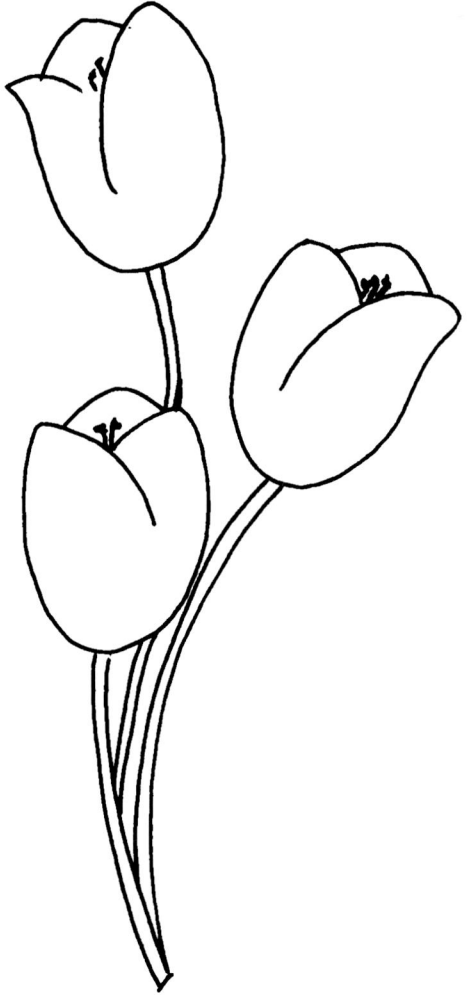

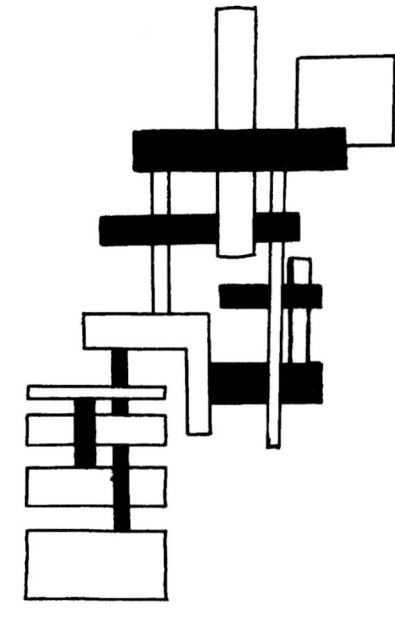

Sketch 8.9 shows a childlike rendition of a raccoon but because of the combination of many different prints used, a degree of sophistication results.

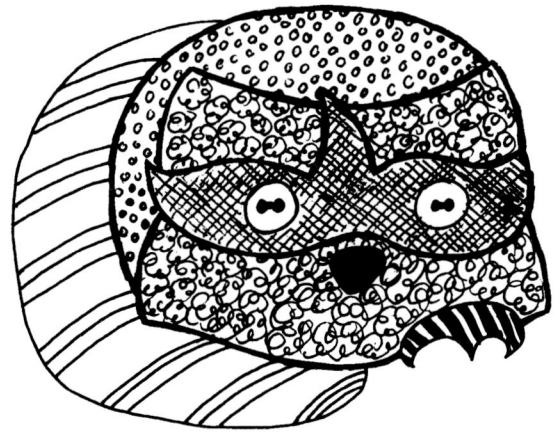

Recognizable shapes are not necessary. These could be simply squares, rectangles, strips in different sizes and colors with a fusible backing pressed on. Arrange these pieces very easily on a sweater or other garment, and rearrange until you like the design. Fuse the finished composition to the garment and you'll discover how easy it is for any non-talented person to be an artist. -sketch 8.8- All of these were kept parallel or perpendicular but could just as well be placed at other angles if that is your preference.

A really simple shape is a circle. Enlarge this one to about 6" in diameter using a saucer to draw around for your pattern. Draw it on a fusible release sheet, rough side up. This circle wouldn't be terribly interesting plunked in the center of a T shirt chest. But distort the

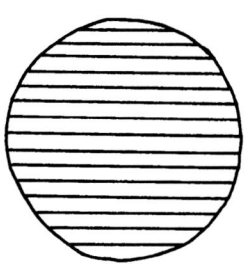fact that it is a mere circle and make it something more interesting. As in sketch 8.10, draw a succession of stripes to cover the whole circle. Fuse this on a non ravely fabric such as a suede. Peel off the paper, cut out the circle and cut apart all the stripes. Arrange them on the garment background in the same order, but spread out in an intriguing design. -sketch 8.11- 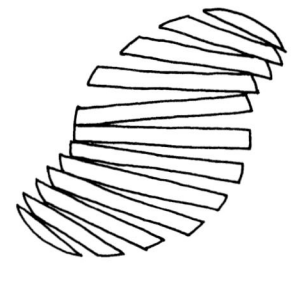Fuse these in place.

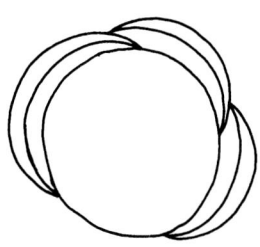Think of this instead as a ball, a piece of sporting equipment. Trim a little off the edges of the circle and fuse those trimmings on the background along with the ball. Sketch 8.12 sort of simulates a basketball and its hoops.

Move the sporting season ahead and, using a punch, produce a golf ball as in -sketch 8.13

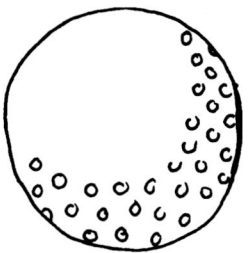

Or my favorite is in the full size, sketch 8.14. Bats for baseball season were drawn in the ball. When cut out the bats are rearranged, overlapping here and there in a pleasant composition.

Appliques you see, can be done by a no-talent, non-artist. This was to get your creative juices flowing, to stimulate the thinking process. Once you follow through, cutting up shapes, simplifying what you see ... you'll discover you can produce some terrific designs by distorting the facts.

Sketch 8.14

Program 9: Creating A Collar

There are times when the pattern you use has a high jewel neck where you would like a collar. If all other features in the pattern are to your liking, the collar you want to add is easy to create.

It is also possible to add a collar to a ready made garment using measurements if no collar presently exists. An extra collar was made on this program to button on to a raincoat which already had its own collar. The reason for a detachable extra collar is to make a related outfit, a coat and dress, using the dress fabric for the button-on coat collar. The obvious easy way to do this is to spread out the attached coat collar on a piece of paper. Trace around the outer three edges. -sketch 9.1-

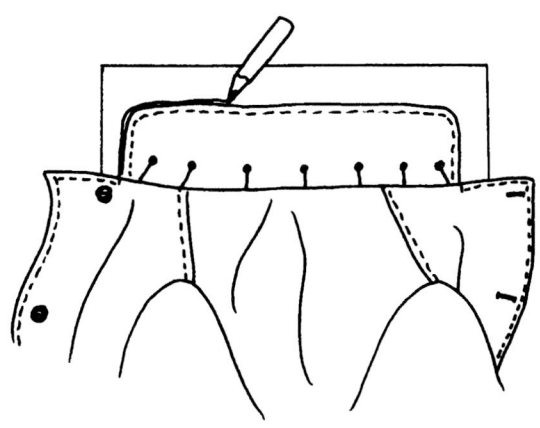

Note the neckline shape which is in this case a simple straight line. If it is shaped, mark the shape by sticking pins through the seamline to pierce the paper beneath. Connecting the pin holes with a pencil will complete the collar outline.

Add seam allowances all around your traced shape. -sketch 9.2- Cut two layers of the

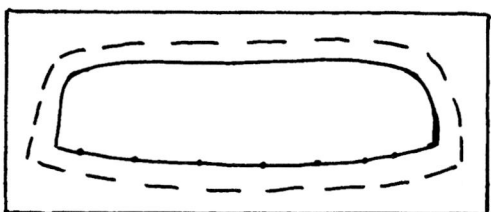

fashion fabric and one layer of fusible interfacing. Fuse this to the wrong side of a fabric layer. Right sides together, pin and stitch all four sides leaving an opening somewhere for turning right side out. Before stitching insert buttonloops at four places between neckline layers. Sketch 9.3 shows the position of these buttonloops between layers as you are stitching.

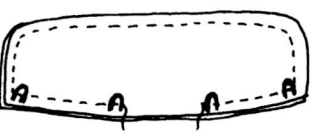

Sketch 9.4 shows their position when the collar is turned right side out.

These loops can be thin tubes made from the collar fabric with a narrow tube turner, commercial elastic buttonloops bought by the yard, or pieces of elastic you cut to size and insert.

On the inside of the coat neckline right below the collar, sew buttons in suitable locations to accommodate the buttonloops. Using a purchased garment for adding a collar is certainly a head start! But making one from scratch is really quite simple.

A full roll collar is the standard and most types of collars are off shoots of this. To make the basic, a neckline pattern measurement is all that is needed. With tape measure on end, curve it around from center front (CF) to shoulder (S). Measure at the 5/8" stitching line, not out at pattern's cut edge. Do not include center or shoulder seams as the garment measurement is all that is needed. Sketch 9.5 illustrates this as well as the position of the back neckline from shoulder to center back (CB).

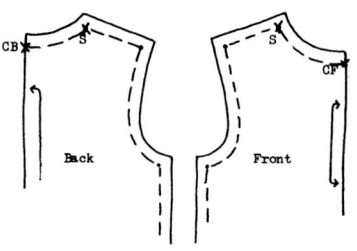

Record these front and back necklines by marking the spaces on a sheet of paper, measuring distances. -sketch 9.6-

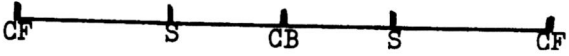

Looking at that line drawn, notice the spacing. It is longer from CF to S than from S to CB. Look at the pattern pieces and see the reason is that the center front is cut down lower than the center back. Look at your side view in the mirror and all this makes sense. Where your chest slopes in from one direction and your neck slopes in from another direction, the point at which they meet is your natural front neckline. To try to wear a neckline higher than this point is miserable and feels like it's choking you. The center back hasn't this problem for your upper back and back neck slope in the same line.

With your neckline drawn what is still needed is the style line and that largely depends on current fashion. On figure 9.7, a mark has been drawn at the center back to signify the desired collar height, the rise or stand. An equal amount up from that will be the collar's edge as it folds over, the fall. A squared off amount was then filled in to complete the collar.

Usually a collar is convertible. This means it can be worn open or buttoned. To allow this to happen gracefully, begin at the shoulder and tape a curved line up to about 1/2" at the center front; refer to figure 9.7. This convex neckline curve is what you almost always see on a standard collar pattern.

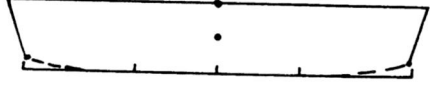

Now with the completed collar, add seam allowances as in sketch 9.8.

The pattern is then ready to cut the fabric layers, and construct the collar. When completed sew it to the garment neckline with or without the facing the commercial pattern includes.

Sketch 9.8 also has a dotted line indicating where the fold line would be when the collar is worn. Frequently this is a cutting line to separate the collar stand and fall.

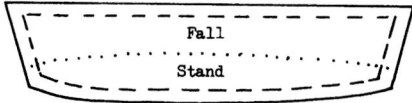

Sketch 9.9 shows them separated, seams added to each. Men's shirts are usually two

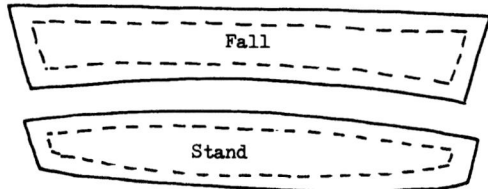

pieces like this for a crisper look and fit. The stand can be used as is for a mandarin collar. The ends will come around exactly to the center front, as sketch 9.10 illustrates.

If you want this collar to come over to the edge which in a blouse or dress will be about 1/2" beyond the center front, add that 1/2" to each end of the collar when you cut it out. That 1/2" is called the extension and provides space for buttons and buttonholes.

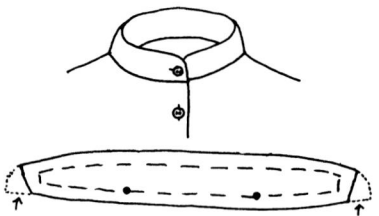

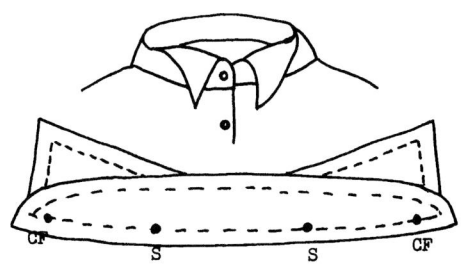

Sketch 9.12 shows a wing tip or tuxedo collar which utilizes the same type collar as in sketch 9.11, but with the wings added from shoulder to center front. You can see how this evolves on and on to develop most collars you would want to design.

A bias collar is a sort of crumpled turtleneck. The neckline measurement is used to cut a rectangle of the same size plus seams. -sketch 9.13-

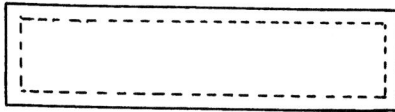

If that is folded so the edges form a right angle, the resulting fold is true bias. -sketch 9.14- This fold line then becomes the grain line to use when cutting fabric.

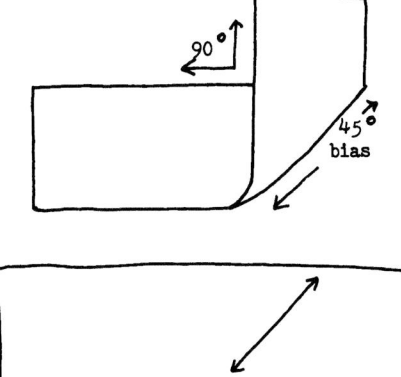

A fitted collar is made by overlapping the pattern back and front shoulders to the stitching line at the neck. -sketch 9.15- Out at the armscye, overlap it an extra 1/2" to slightly tighten up the collar style line so it will not ripple.

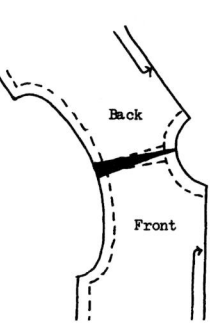

Trace the neckline as well as a little of the center front and center back. The style lines which you draw yourself, without the pattern, determines what the collar will look like. The group sketches of 9.16 show the collar patterns and their finished results.

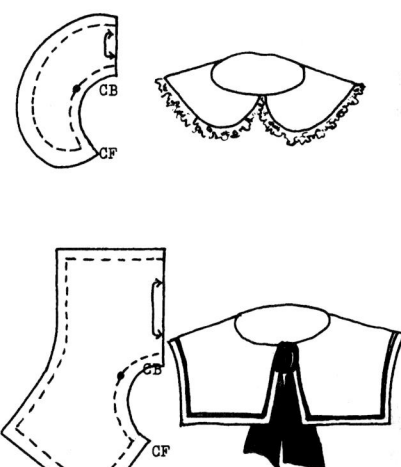

Even the big shaggy fringed collar shown in the one layer coat on programs 5 and 6 was made from a fitted collar pattern as you can see by referring back to those pages.

The more you know about how patterns work and how you can change them, the easier and more logical sewing becomes.

Program 10: Turtle Quilt

I know this little girl who just does not like to take a nap. As a special inducement I've made her a gift ... a turtle quilt. The point of this is that just as a turtle carries his house on his back, this pillow is the storage enclosing its own attached quilt. Since it's a combination quilt and pillow, some call it a quillow!

Although these directions are for a child's quilt, reinterpret the idea on adult terms. It could be a family room afghan or a car robe. Think about a carry-along for a football game either to sit on or to open up and cuddle into if the thermometer dips.

-Sketch 10.1- Decide on the size of your quilt. Cut two layers of fabric and one layer of quilt batting. Stack batt on the bottom, two fabric layers on top, their right sides together. Hold together with a few pins.

 -Sketch 10.2- By serger or sewing machine, stitch all around edge leaving an opening for turning at one end. If you have a serger, that's the quickest choice. It does a beautiful job and trims off excess all in one simple operation. This way it's done so quickly, you could mass produce a bunch of these for the club bazaar!

-Sketch 10.3- Reaching between fabric layers, gently push corners out square and turn the quilt right side out. Straighten all edges and press them. Tuck open seam allowances to inside and press and stitch the opening closed.

-Sketch 10.4- Pin at regular intervals all over the quilt to hold all layers smoothly together. Safety pins in a rather large size work best for this. Work on a flat surface to keep it all smooth and square. Every place you have a pin, about every 4" - 6", stitch the layers together with some decorative stitch your machine will do. This is accomplishing the same job as tufting. Remove each pin as you stitch in its place.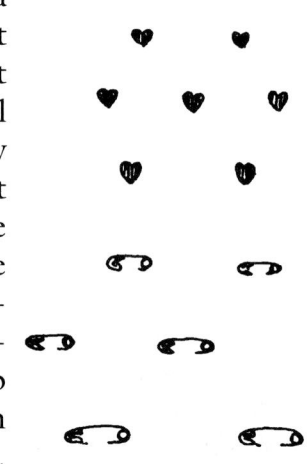

-Sketch 10.5- Make a pillow with both sides complete but unstuffed. If you think a more "plump" look would be a good idea, construct same as the quilt with a batting layer between. The outside edge may remain plain or embellished with a ruffle, piping or ruching. Directions for these edge trims will be explained later.

-Sketch 10.6- Center the pillow on the quilt with the side down which you have chosen for the finished (when folded up) side. For the one pictured in the colored pages, that meant the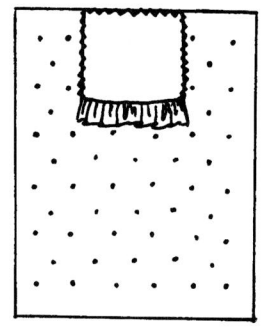

turtle side was down. If there will be a ruffle it should all be tucked under as the pillow is pinned in place around three sides, lower side left open. Stitch all around. When making mine, at about this point I decided my pillow was too small to fold the quilt into. To enlarge it, I therefore cut a strip of bias and with a bias tape maker, folded and pressed the edges under. Sketch 10.7 shows how this bias was then stitched over the ruffle edge to anchor to the quilt, but also to enlarge the pillow by 2" or more on three sides. This made the necessary space to 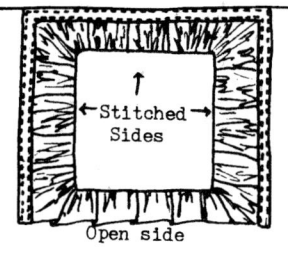 accommodate the folded up quilt. If one way won't work, you can usually create an alternative!

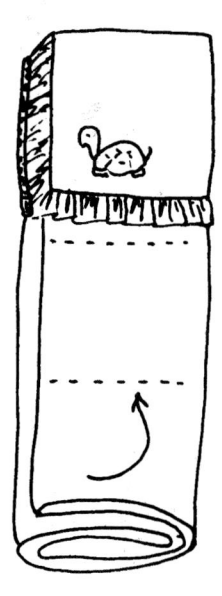 -Sketch 10.8- To fold the quilt for storage, turn the pillow right side out and the quilt automatically begins to conform. The two sides are forced to fold into the center up inside of the pillow. Neatly smooth them in thirds all the way to the lower end (refer to dotted line on sketch 10.8). Starting at the bottom, fold up approximately the size of the pillow. Then fold again and it all tucks up inside the pillow. -sketch 10.9-

Three suggestions follow to finish the edges of the quilt pillow, or to finish any pillow.

A ruffle of the same or harmonizing fabric is probably best made of a double fabric layer so that the pillow can be used on either side. This fabric is folded in half, wrong sides together, then gathered. -sketch 10.10- Cut this twice the desired width of the finished ruffle plus seam allowances.

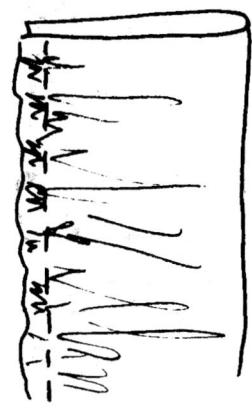

If the backside will never show it would be alright to make the ruffle one layer and hem the outside edge with a hemmer foot, topstitching it in place. Another finish would be satin stitching the raw edge on a sewing machine. A similar look, quicker still, is to make a rolled hem on the serger.

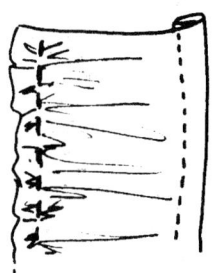

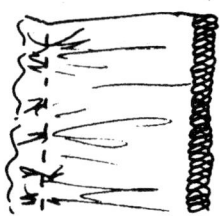

Eyelet or lace, pre-ruffled or purchased flat and you ruffle it yourself, are also possibilities.

For any of these measure the pillow edge. That circumference measurement times 2 or 3, depending on fabric weight, will be the length of the fabric strip used to make a ruffle.

Stitch the ends together so it makes a big ring. Be sure to not twist it before joining. The double thickness type is stitched right sides together, then folded wrong sides together so it will all be finished on the outside. Single thickness fabric or eyelet should be joined with a French seam or serger rolled hem so both sides look right.

Gathering can be done easily with the use of a gathering foot. Tighten the thread tension and lengthen the stitch for closer gathers. Figure out on a scrap the correct amount.

If you have a ruffler, this is the perfect place to use it and it also can be adjusted for more or less fullness.

Other possibilities are two rows of long stitches near the raw edge, drawn up to the proper fullness. Zigzagging over a heavy thread like perle cotton, then drawing up the heavy cord is fine in the absence of the specialty feet. -sketch 10.12

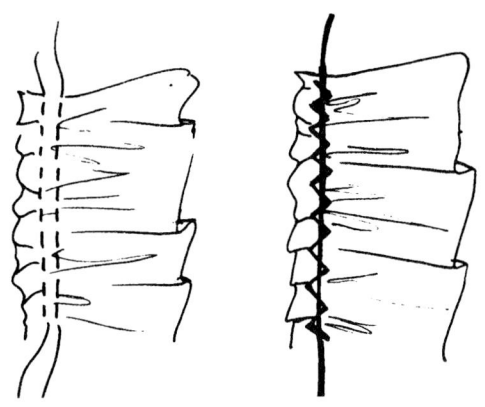

When this flounce is gathered down to the size of the pillow edge, pin it in place on the right side of the pillow. Raw edges will be together at the outside, finished ruffle edge toward the pillow center. If needed to hold excess fullness down and out of the way, tape across corners so they cannot get out of control. -sketch 10.13-

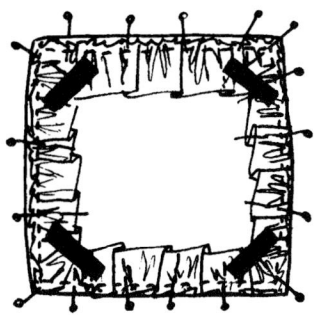

At this point you may want to machine baste the ruffle at its edge to more easily control it. If that seems unnecessary, then directly put the pillow top in place, right sides together, and machine stitch all around the edge through all three layers at once. Leave an opening somewhere for turning right side out. When turned, the flounce will be in its correct position. Close the opening by hand or by machine.

Another edging is a piping. This is a strip of fabric 1 1/2" wide cut either on the straight or on the bias. On the bias it would be softer and smoother, if this would be a factor. Fold it over a heavy cord or fat yarn, wrong sides together. Using a cording foot or a zipper foot, stitch close to the cord to encase and hold it. -sketch 10.14-

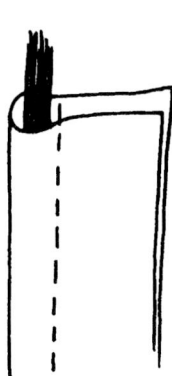

Apply it to the pillow in the same way as the ruffle, finished fold of the piping toward the center, raw edges outward. Clip the corners so they will lie flat. Overlap the start and finish tapering the ends outward. -sketch 10.15-

A ruched edge is very attractive on pillows and made almost the same way. You need for this a very fat soft roping found by the yard in fabric or upholstery shops. It is puffy batting encased in a mesh covering. Your fabric will need to be cut quite wide, maybe 4" or 5" depending on the size of your rope. Cut this fabric strip about twice the length of the pillow circumference as it will be gathered up quite full when stitched.

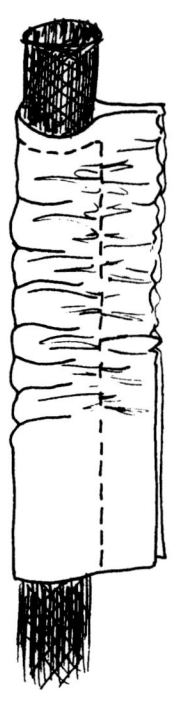

As sketch 10.16 shows, stitch across one end of the fabric-wrapped rope to hold it firmly in place, then stitch down the strip length. Again, a zipper foot is helpful BUT do not stitch too close to the rope. You want the fabric to be a little loose on it. Every 6" or so as you stitch, stop, needle down in fabric to hold it firmly. Pull the roping toward you with one hand as you use the other hand to gather the fabric up on the rope behind the needle. It is then applied between pillow layers same as narrow piping.

The same techniques can be used to make pillows, not for housing a quilt, but just as individual pillows to be filled with purchased pillowforms. The only difference here is that it is wise to make an opening so that the pillow can be removed to wash the cover. Two ideas here might be zipping the lower edge or like sketch 10.17, making a two-piece backing overlapping at the center for pillow removal. Doing this on a large scale will produce a pillow sham for decoratively holding large bed pillows.

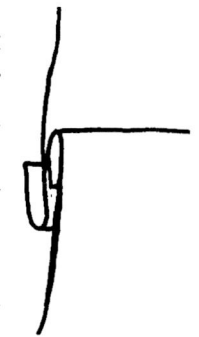

Sometimes these pillow covers are made about 2" or 3" larger on all sides than the pillow which will fill them. After finishing and turning right side out they are topstitched down to the size of the pillow, thus creating a flange edging. A variety of shapes and sizes used together makes a pretty grouping.

If instead of using fabric by the yard, you use flat bedsheets to get the fabric you want ... here is the yardage each will produce. This is equating it with 45" fabric widths:

Twin sheet 66" x 96" about 3 1/2 yards
Full size   81" x 96"   4 1/2 yards
Queen   90" x 102"   5 1/2 yards
King   108" x 102"   6   yards

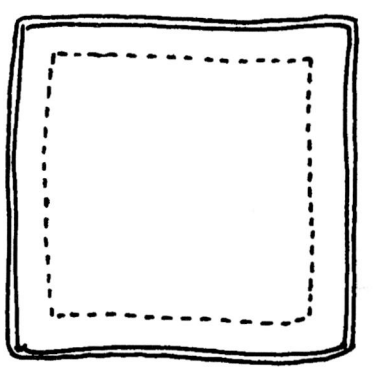

Sketch 10.18

Program 11: Make It Special

Recently someone said of what I was wearing, "That looks like it took a lot of time. I thought your thing was quick and easy!" How could anyone have me so wrong? If it can be done quickly, fine. We all find ourselves very short on time. But if to get a quality job it turns out to be quite time consuming, I can live with that. No one needs just one more garment to cover her back unless she recently gained 100 pounds. If I'm going to put the time, money and effort into any sewing, I want to make it special.

This involves getting fabrics that really appeal to you. Shop carefully and only buy those which sing to you, which make you feel wonderful just to look at them. Think carefully about how they would best be made up. If a pattern like that seems non-existent, make your own.

Begin with a pattern which has simple, fitted lines and it will convert to almost anything. The pattern I used for a particular dress, the one demonstrated on program 11, is actually a fitted jacket pattern which has an enormous front overlap. That is immediately folded out of the way. A center front line is always marked on a pattern, so folding to that line is simple. -sketch 11.1- There is nothing magic about this pattern except that it has a fitted shoulder and sleeve area. Many of today's patterns have dropped shoulders, flat sleeve caps and oversize fit. For the dress I wanted to make, the fitted look for a starting point is a prerequisite. A dress pattern may seem more logical, but patterns are so wonderfully versatile that the feature (shoulder fit) is more important than the type (dress rather than jacket).

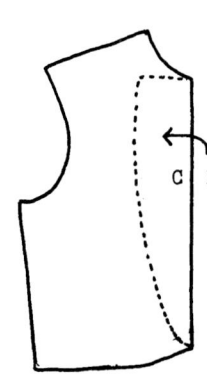

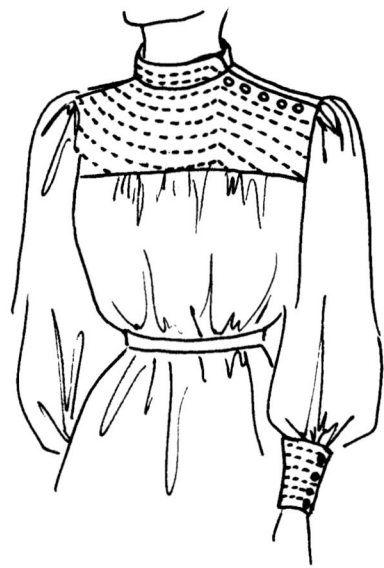

-Sketch 11.2- Start with a picture of what you are making. It may be a mental picture (if you feel confident enough to work from this) or a rough sketch of the features you want to put together, or a magazine clipping you want to copy verbatim. We'll begin with the top of this pattern and move down to show its development.

I want a mandarin collar. The jacket is collarless. Refer back to program 9 to design a collar just by measuring the front and back necklines. Make the stand part of a basic full roll collar. Curve the lower edge (neck edge) and this will fit whether the neck opening is front, back or side. -sketch 11.3- It is built to overlap 1/2" at the joining so that it comes out to the closure edge. That means it is actually cut 1" longer than the neckline plus seams.

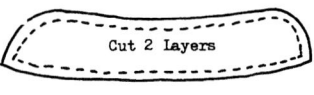

The bodice front and back are cut in two for the yoke addition. Try the pattern front on your body to determine where the yoke line will be. This one is about 5" below the center front neckline so the pattern is folded horizontally at that point and placed on the fabric. -sketch 11.4-

Although this is on a fold making a double fabric layer, two of these are needed of the fashion fabric and one layer of a quilt batting between them. In the interest of saving time I might fold the fabric again to make four layers and cut out both at once. You can also just cut a second time if you prefer for the other layer. Notice the dotted line added at the bottom. This is the seam allowance which must be added to sew it to the lower bodice.

The lower bodice then needs fullness to gather up and stitch to the yoke. How much fullness? The common sense way is to gather fabric in your hands as you hold it against your body to judge the effect. I moved my center front 2" away from the fabric fold to add 4" of fullness. -sketch 11.5- Add the seam allowance at the top to stitch to the yoke. The original jacket pattern came to the waistline. 8" needs to be added for this two-piece dress to be tucked into the skirt.

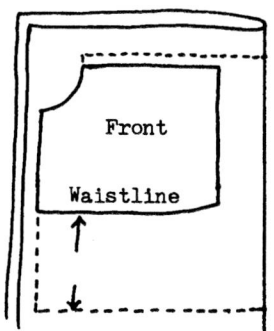

The bodice back will be treated the very same way as the front, with one small exception. Remember this will button on the left shoulder. That will require a 1" underlap on the left shoulder back. The easiest way to do this is to add a 1" extension up on the shoulders when cutting the four layers. -sketch 11.6- Then when opened up simply trim that one inch off the right shoulder, leaving the left intact. -sketch 11.7- Later, when finished, buttons will stitch to that yoke extension.

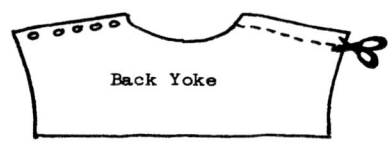

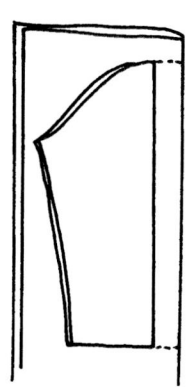

The sleeves have fullness added by the same technique as the lower bodice ... moving them over from the fold. -sketch 11.8- Fold the paper pattern in half vertically. The shape of the sleeve cap back and front will differ an insignificant amount. The length might be made a little shorter depending on the wrist treatment. The one shown has a deep cuff so some shortening is probably wise.

The cuff is 5" high. Measure your wrist, then your forearm 5" above and the difference will be considerable. Cut a paper rectangle your larger measurement and add 3 1/2" to that for seams, overlap and ease. -sketch 11.9-

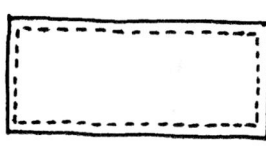

Then make several little folds in the bottom, tapering out to nothing at the top. Pleat as many times as is necessary until the wrist measures 3 1/2" larger than yours. Tape across to hold the pleats stable. With this pattern, cut 4 layers of fabric. -sketch 11.10-

From clothing quilting fleece, cut two cuff layers, one yoke front, one yoke back, one collar, and you're finished. Wasn't that easy to make these simple changes enabling you to design whatever you please or copy anything you see? This is one way to make it special, having anything you want, unlimited by pattern availability.

When you sew this, there will be no guide sheet. Stretch your mind a little by thinking through which process will logically come first, which second, etc. You might even make a list of procedures and prioritize the processes.

Also to make it special think of unusual techniques which would only be found in the expensive designer fashions. On this it will be the rows of machine quilting instead of interfacing used in obvious places. The middle price clothing, if quilted, would be symmetrically balanced stitching lines going in predictable directions. Let's therefore be different and follow other paths. Sketch 11.11 represents one idea, off-balance, which shows a little more originality. Following the shoulder-neckline instead of the lower yokeline, flavors this more interestingly.

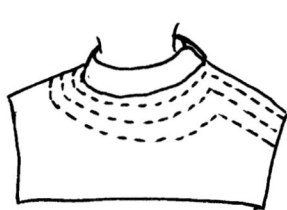

The skirt is simply gathered and attached to the waistband. The waistline deserves a distinctive look also. Since the waistband is ordinary, a spectacular belt might be in order.

The basic technique for this belt is found in my books "Fused Belts" and in "The Sewing Connection Series I" so I won't repeat the whole process here. Briefly, the belt backing uses the dress fabric fused in place for its covering. The outer side of the belt is covered in Ultra Suede® shapes whose colors duplicate those in the dress fabric print. One of the delightful benefits of sewing is that everyone can be an artist. You need have no color sense whatever if you just start with a print fabric you like, and borrow the colors a fiber artist has put together. The several colors of belt suede I just happened to have, but if not, they can be purchased in fabric stores. I would have found them one way or another.

I was tempted to embellish this belt with some objects from nature. The two choices I considered were 1. An oyster shell because its shape fit in so appropriately with the print which hinted of undersea objects. It had a really interesting shape which would have been a challenge finding a way to attach it. 2. An interesting flat piece of driftwood, because its weathered, mellow brown color echoed the same color in the fabric print. I actually chose neither because the suede pieces provided about all the embellishment one belt could use.

A simple way for a non-artist to cut these shapes would be to trace them from the fabric on fusible web release sheets. Fuse these to the backs of suede pieces, cut them out, peel off the paper backing. Adjust all these on the belt until you find the best arrangement. Cover with a press cloth and fuse on a press or with an iron. Then straight stitch all the edges for lasting permanency.

The belt pictured in sketch 11.12 was not actually a tracing. The curvy shapes of the suede pieces, however, hint of the fabric design and therefore blend in with it. Stitch the two belt layers together to complete the project.

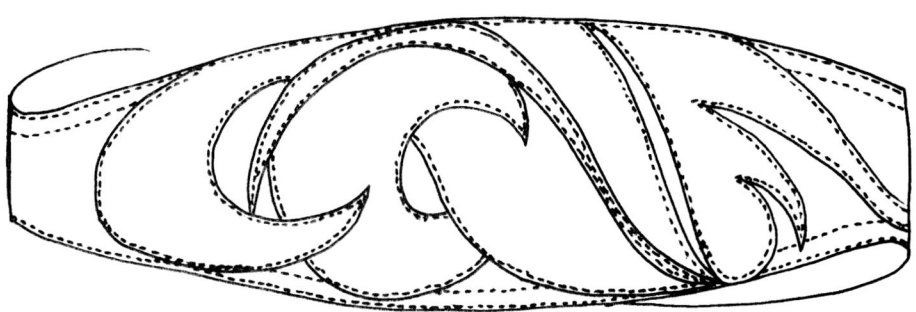

This outfit wasn't necessarily made in a hurry, but it was very enjoyable to make. One of the fun things about it is that it is unique, one of a kind, and nowhere will you see another exactly like it. This is true of any of your sewing when you do some original thinking and make it special.

Burda 5006 is the jacket pattern from which this dress is adapted.

Program 12: The Little Black Dress

Viewers of The Sewing Connection write me lots of letters and several wanted a little advice on:

- What can I put on in the morning to take me through the evening?
- What can I wear when I want to feel just right ... not over or under dressed and I don't know what others will have on?
- What would be right for this one big occasion which I can then keep wearing in different ways?

The answer to all the above is the little black dress. No matter that magazines from time to time say that color is everywhere, forget black! Rarely would there be a time when that little black dress isn't one of your best wardrobe friends.

Black is a color some find difficult to wear. If so, substitute a more flattering dark neutral and it will still give the same effect. Perhaps on you, navy, charcoal, or chocolate brown would bring out your skin tones in a more complimentary way.

The fabric is another consideration. My basic black is a tissue faille for three-season wear but I also like a black linen for summer, a black wool jersey in winter, a black velvet for cold weather. Think not only season but also figure flattery. A soft fabric but one with a little weight to drape nicely is good on most bodies. "Basic" is different for everyone. A friend of mine has chosen for her basic black a knit with lycra so that it hugs her figure very closely, following every curve. It looks wonderful on her, but it's not for everyone!

Think also about light reflection. Matte fabrics which absorb light are wearer-friendly. All my black things are in this category and much easier to wear for any woman. The shiny fabrics (like satin) are best on very good figures who can afford to wear them ... no bumps and bulges to highlight.

The cut of the dress must be thought out. Will the neckline be high for day or night versatility? How about a high front and a plunging back ... a jacket over it for day wear? Even a low front surplice neckline fills in nicely with a scarf. Perhaps versatility isn't a consideration and a slip-dress is more of what you need, straps only or strapless. Sleeveless? Cap sleeves? Short or long? This is terrific to be a home sewer and choose exactly what you want. Put together all the features you like and would be best for your purposes. Is the bodice shapely with a fitted waistline or will it be a shift and hang straight with no accented waistline, if yours is better unaccented? That shift would be best worn quite short (a long shapeless shift merely looks dowdy) and the perfect chance to accent great legs. Will the skirt be fitted or full? -sketch 12.1-

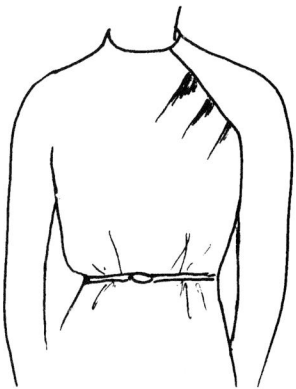

There might be a perfect pattern for you to encompass all the features you prefer. If not, program 11 gave you some insight into how easy it is to change a pattern. Just find one somewhat close and change parts of it to conform. Or combine different pattern pieces. Measure the stitching lines of the adjoining seams and adjust one or the other to fit.

Does your basic have a high neckline which you would like to adjust lower? Redesigning this on the flat paper pattern on the table is difficult as you don't know exactly where that new line will turn out on your body. The easier way might be to cut out the fabric as the pattern indicates. Stitch the shoulder seams together and press open. Put the partially constructed dress on, pin neck closing and a couple of pins on each side seam to hold it in place. With a piece of yarn or cord or a long chain necklace, outline the shape of the neckline you would like to have. This way you will know exactly how it will work in relation to your lingerie straps.

-Sketch 12.2- Trace that outline with pins or with a chalkline. Take the dress off and add 5/8" above your marked line for a seam

allowance. Cut away the neck part you don't want. -sketch 12.3- Use that cut-off part as a template to put on your paper pattern. The facing for the new neckline would then start at the cut-off edge and extend down into the bodice 3". If the new neckline you design is very low, taping

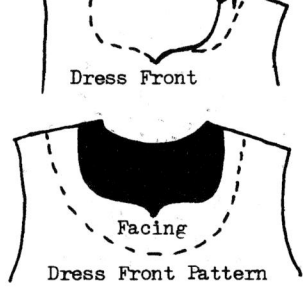

the edge may be necessary to keep it from gaping away from the body. This may be a narrow twill tape, seam tape cut in half, or thin selvage. Ease the low neck stitching line unto this tape as you pin, then stitch the tape to the fabric wrong side. If you do this, cut the facing off a little shorter, proportionately, at the shoulder ends so it will fit just right.

-sketch 12.4-

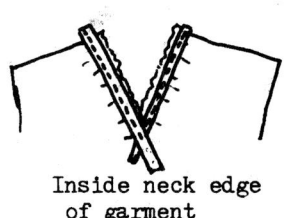

Inside neck edge of garment

The little puckers which show in the sketch can then be eased in with a steam pressing. If using fusible interfacing, it is easier to only cut out the interfacing with the facing pattern. Fuse this to the uncut fabric backside which will be the facing. Then it's really an easy matter to cut around it for the facing.

The pattern I used for my basic black dress said not only on the envelope, but on each and every pattern piece, "For moderate stretch knits only." Looking at the envelope picture, I could see no reason for this restriction. It looked like it would work up beautifully in the woven soft tissue faille I planned to use. Sometimes when patterns stipulate knits only, it is possible to use a woven on the bias so it has some stretch. To these you may have to add zippers since you can't depend on the knit stretch to give ease in pulling on and off. When patterns suggest the fabric which would work best, they usually have a good reason and it's wise to heed their advice. If you do something contrary to this, think it through very carefully.

Measure the bust and hip areas to be sure these are ample plus ease. Measure the wrist of a long sleeve to see if it is wide enough for your hand to slide through. If it is too tight for this but you want a slim wrist look when wearing, add a little to the seam allowances for leaving a few inches open, turning under facings twice (this would include an interfacing) and making a button and buttonhole closing.
-sketch 12.5-

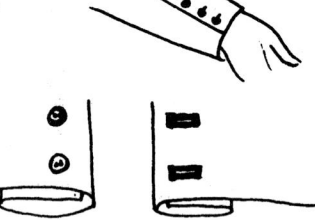

I find that on mine it all works out well in a straight cut woven. Even the back zipper was long enough to slip over when dressing. Why the pattern stipulated "knits only" therefore remains a mystery.

Consider whether this fabric should be lined, underlined, or used in the single layer. Leave it a single layer if:
- it is already heavy enough and no more bulk is desired;
- it won't stretch, sag, or get seat sprung since the fabric is stable;
- it is a simple style and needs no support layers to bolster construction details such as pockets;
- the fabric can be hemmed to itself and look terrific on the outside.

Underlining is when you cut a lining layer from the same pattern and staystitch this to the backside of the fashion fabric layer before construction of the seams. It is a good idea to use this if:
- the fabric needs some "beefing up" to make it look and feel richer as it seems flimsy on its own;
- it needs the extra layer for stability to hold it in shape;
- it is needed to provide a backing for construction details;
- the hems should be hemmed to the underlining, handstitches excluded from the outer layer, so nothing tacky shows on the outside.

If your fashion fabric has some stretch whether woven or knit, put it on the underside when staystitching. Lining fabrics are very stable so with this layer on top, no stretching out will occur. If you staystitch with a stretchy fabric on top, it will probably stretch out a little when the presser foot pushes it along. This is something you want to avoid.

A lining layer is one which is constructed separately and only attaches to the dress at neckline, around zipper, at waistline if there is a horizontal seam, and at sleeve hems. The lower skirt hem hangs free and is hemmed separately. Its purpose is to give a more luxurious look mainly, rather than being utilitarian. If in doubt about which treatment would be best, go look at expensive ready-to-wear which has been made from similar fabric. This can be a terrific education as you sometimes realize several support layers have been used to produce the proper elegance.

A designer hem I've noticed, which is invisible from the outside, is merely serging the lower raw edge before hemming. Just any kind of serger thread cannot be used for very delicate fabrics as it is too heavy and it shows through to the outside when pressed. A very light thread must be used for this. The large spools of rayon machine embroidery thread might work well as this is very fine. A serger thread sold on cones which is finer than most is Venus® and this gives very little bulk.

The hem on the expensive designer dress was finished as in sketch 12.6. Folding the

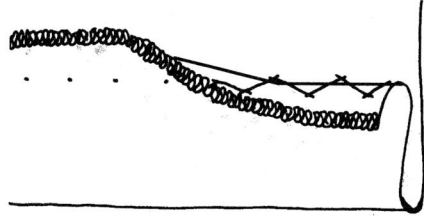

serged edge down 1/2" or so, hand catch stitch between layers. Don't pull the thread too tight or dimples will show on the outside. When pressing do not mash the serged edge into the fabric. That would leave unattractive impressions if the fabric is delicate, even if the serger thread is light weight.

If there is no topstitching elsewhere on this dress, the zipper should possibly not be topstitched in either. Two other alternatives which are now done on expensive dresses are hand picking a standard zipper or using an invisible zipper. The latter is stitched in by machine but underneath so no stitching shows on the outside. All that does show is the zipper tab, which means color selection is important. Color selection in the invisible type is also quite limited so it may be necessary to do some creative camouflage on the tab. Think of painting it if possible, or covering it with a tassel, an interesting fabric or suede shape glued around it, or perhaps "jewels" glued all over it.

If a standard zipper will be used and hand picked, the outside really shows nothing but the slight dimple produced from the little bit -sketch 11.7- of thread showing every time a backstitch is taken. Working from the outside, bring the needle up about every 1/4" and pull the thread up taut. Then put the needle in again from the topside, about 1/16" behind that spot as shown in sketch 12.7.

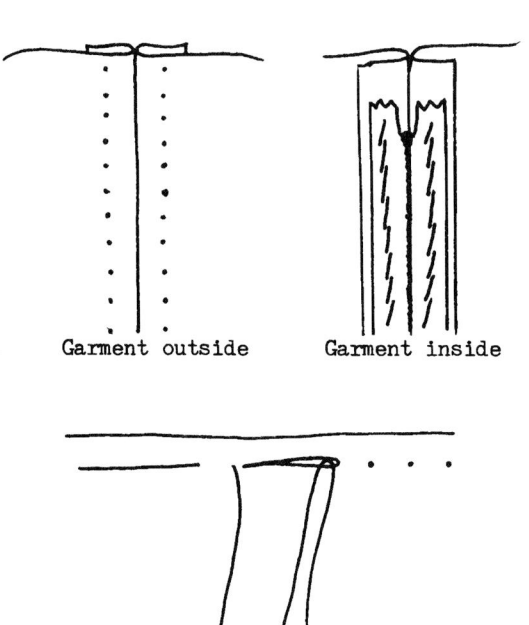

This zipper should be set down low enough, if it is a back neck zipper, to accommodate a floating snap or hook and eye at the very top. One of these brings the two edges together much more attractively than just the zipper top can do alone. Sketch 12.8 shows

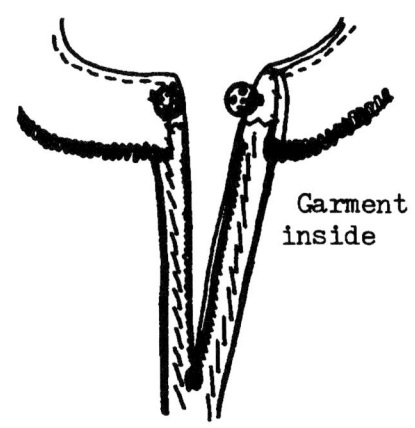

how one part of the snap is sewn completely on the underside of the dress. The other part is only stitched through one of its holes, the other three holes staying free, and it hangs off the garment.

The finished dress then can give you endless daytime versatility as it is worn with jackets, scarves, collars or changes of jewelry to give it a different look every time.

To turn it into evening, look into program 13.

The black dress worn was made from Vogue 7914 out of a tissue faille and underlined.

Program 13: Night On The Town

Using the little black dress as the beginning, what can be added to make it festive? To turn day into night? The added extra might be in the form of a stole. To find the right measurements I went through a bunch of magazine clippings to see how they looked on models who had them draped around their shoulders, over their arms and hanging down at the sides. Pinning two tape measures together and draping them the same way as the photographs, I discovered many inches shorter would be better. 2 1/2 yards long turned out to be just right and 22" wide looked the same as in magazines. Refer to the color photographs in the book center and the stole will be photographed in a royal blue silk brocade with medallions and a silver metallic lining.

Cut the two layers of fabric the same size, 2 1/2 yards by 22". Stitch the two long sides, right sides together. -sketch 13.1-

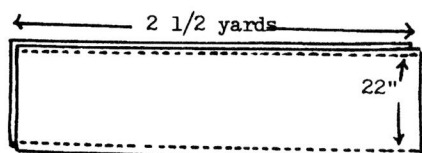

Turn right side out and press the seams. Using some heavy thread such as buttonhole twist for the upper thread in the sewing machine, run two large-stitch rows at each end. -sketch 13.2- Draw up the cords as tightly as you possibly can, really pulling hard.

-sketch 13.3- This is the reason for using such heavy thread as it must be very strong to avoid breaking. Wind them around several times and tie knots to hold. These ends will be very thick and  stiff. Cut a rectangle of lining fabric about 5" x 6". -sketch 13.4-

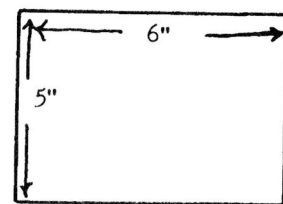

At one end of this piece fold over the end, then fold it lengthwise in half. Wrap it tightly around the gathered stole end, all raw edges together, and stitch by hand. Push the needle back and forth through the mass securing well from every angle about 1" from the ends. A needle gripper may be needed to pull the needle through on each stitch. -sketch 13.5-

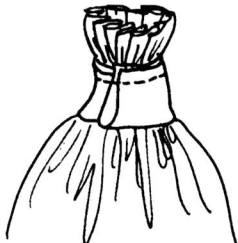

Peel that sleeve down over the end as in sketch 13.6. Gather finished end with the needle so it all pulls together tightly. To the center of this little flower, stitch a fat tassel. -sketch 13.7-

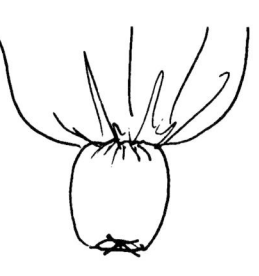

This tassel may be purchased if you can find the right size in the right color. Another alternative is to make one yourself.

Use a heavy cord to make a tassel, as I made one of silver sewing thread and, wound around a card about 300 times, it was still skimpy! Use something like Madeira Decor, ribbon floss, Candlelight or any of the heavy novelty threads suitable for flatlocking on a serger ... soft and fat. Using a cardboard or anything stiff and about 5" long, wrap the cord around about 75 to 100 times, or more if necessary to make it generously full. Tie it at the top with another cord, and cut them all apart at the bottom. -sketch 13.8- With another cord tie again where arrow points in sketch 13.9.

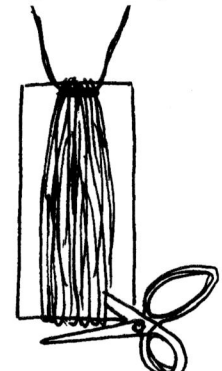
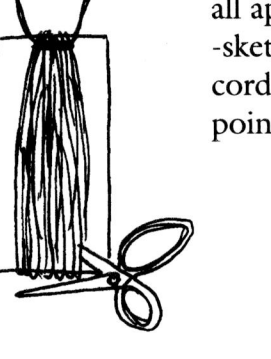

Sketch 13.11

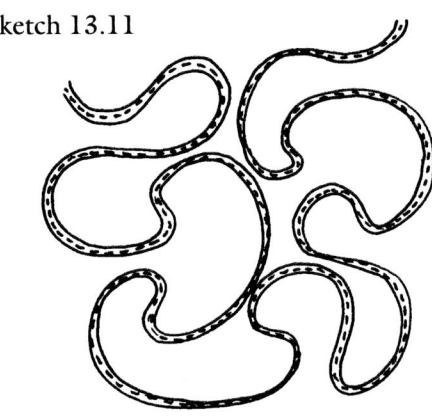

So many of these same cords or strings of pearls or strings of sequins can be couched on for decorative effects. For this procedure a special foot will be helpful in holding the cord in place while you stitch over it. This wide braid foot can be purchased at your sewing machine dealer. Sketch 13.10 shows how a zigzag stitch will hold cord or pearls in place. Too many stitches detract from smooth cord so the last illustration uses less thread crossings in the blind hem stitch.

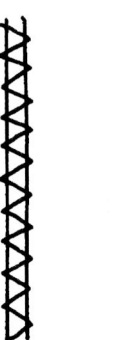

Passamenterie was popular at the turn of the century and it is enjoying a resurgence recently, embellishing jackets or dresses or accessories. This is a design made of cording, not stitched in straight rows, but meandering in and out in curvy lines and very complicated directions. It also needs the wide braid foot to hold the cord in place while it is couched to the fabric. -sketch 13.11- Try this with cords or with soutache braid, first practicing on a scrap of fabric before your actual garment. It may need some tear-away stabilizer under the fabric to avoid puckering.

Sequined fabrics are amazingly easy to handle. Cut out as any other fabric and the sequins, which are mainly plastic, will cause no problems. Sew together in a shallow seam, right sides together. A zigzag stitch then will hold the seam edges together to prevent fraying. Facings should be of another fabric, a plain silky fabric which adds extra bulk to a seam.

An interesting way to finish off hem edges when you don't actually want to turn up a hem is through the use of a fusible tricot interfacing. Shown on air was an all over sequined fabric. The rows of colored glitz were applied in a flame stitch design. To destroy the pattern by simply hemming up in a straight line would have been a waste. Its creator instead stitched a 4" strip of fusible tricot interfacing to the hem, right sides together, following the flame design. Trim off close to the stitching line and clip at the point of each V. -sketch 13.12-

Turn the interfacing to the wrong side and fuse to the garment inside using a terry towel under the sequined garment and a press cloth on top. Try this pressing first on a scrap to be sure sequins do not melt. -sketch 13.13-

An unstructured jacket in a metallic fabric is a definite evening look to top a basic black dress. The variety of metallic fabrics available is endless. Their price tags will fit any budget. -sketch 13.14-

Directions for the one shown on this show were at the end of The Sewing Connection Series II so they will not be repeated here. This is working with a very soft knit tricot, metallic printed, and actually poses no problems. It is even washable and carries the added bonus of a tiny price tag.

The opposite end of the price range was shown in a striped metallic fabric which has yet to be made up into a garment. Typically, the higher the price, the more thought and planning is demanded before cutting into the fabric. When so much is at stake, take these precautions:

- Explore every corner of ready-to-wear, catalogues, magazines to discover the perfect style worthy of the magnificent fabric.
- Find a pattern that is close to what you want and make all necessary changes in details.
- Make that up in another fabric as a test pattern to perfect the fit. Not necessarily a throw-away, this can be a wearable garment but in a fabric of lesser cost.
- Perfect the pattern and lay it on the fabric. If it is not a solid, consider very carefully where the designs will be located on the body, where everything must be matched. Think through all possibilities before cutting.
- With the scraps test all stitching techniques to find the perfect methods. Test iron temperature, steam or dry, presscloths, etc. to have no tragic accidents on the garments. Testing every question on a scrap gives all the best answers.

The emerald green jacket, a silk satin jacquard, had been in my fabric stash for 36 years. Does that classify it as an "antique" fabric? It has been very silent all these years and only recently spoke to me to let me know what it wants to be. A good year for Oriental opulence, it's time had finally come.
-sketch 13.15-

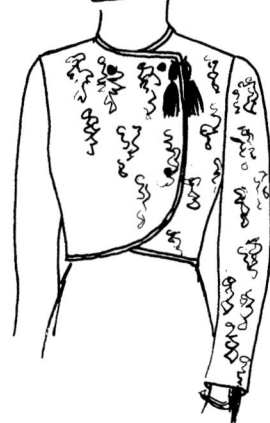

The first inclination in shopping for the lining was to match the green, but this thought was quickly discarded. In the woven design is a flaming pink bird. The happier decision is to think "this is evening"! Pull out all the stops. Make it bright and festive. Make it a party.

The lining is therefore a flashing pink and the same fabric binds all edges for a startling accent. The same color in a heavy silken cord makes tassels which tie the upper corner in place. Buttonholes would break up the fabric design and add nothing. Because of the wide overlap at the front closing the jacket cannot be worn open so will always be fastened. Snaps were therefore used to support and position the front lapovers. These are in the places the dots in sketch 13.15 show but in reality, on the jacket they are between layers and not visible.

A variety of belts and jewelry, all of which say evening, can be used on this little black dress to change the look every time it is worn. The trims department at fabric shops carry big lines of sequined appliques which can be stitched or fused to a garment. If only a temporary usage is planned, Sticky Stuff® painted on the backside will allow wearing on a garment, then taking off to switch from the sequined motif one time, to a lacy snowflake the next wearing. The choices are limitless for transforming a simple black dress to anything your mood of the moment dictates.

All these choices are what make you a designer and keep you sewing to have anything you want ... on your terms. Sewing is YOUR connection to the world of fashion. Enjoy it!

Sticky Stuff® is a pressure-sensitive paint-on found in shops or from Clotilde's catalog.

Sequined garments courtesy of Sue Hausmann, Director of Education Viking Sewing Machine Company